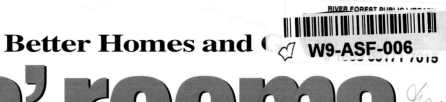

Better Homes and G...

kids' rooms
decorating ideas
under $50

RIVER FOREST PUBLIC LIBRARY
735 LATHROP
RIVER FOREST, IL 60305

WITHDRAWN

Meredith® Books
Des Moines, Iowa

Kids' Rooms—Decorating Ideas Under $50
Editor: Vicki Christian
Contributing Writers: Jana Finnegan, Carol Linnan, Jil Severson
Graphic Designer: Todd Hanson, David Jordan
Copy Chief: Terri Fredrickson
Publishing Operations Manager: Karen Schirm
Edit and Design Production Coordinator: Mary Lee Gavin
Editorial Assistants: Kaye Chabot, Kairee Mullen
Marketing Product Managers: Aparna Pande, Isaac Petersen, Gina Rickert, Stephen Rogers,
    Brent Wiersma, Tyler Woods
Book Production Managers: Pam Kvitne, Marjorie J. Schenkelberg, Rick von Holdt, Mark Weaver
Contributing Copy Editor: Joyce Gemperlein
Contributing Proofreaders: Sarah Enticknap, Elizabeth Havey, Heidi Johnson, Allison Merrill
Indexer: Jana Finnegan

Meredith® Books
Executive Director, Editorial: Gregory H. Kayko
Executive Director, Design: Matt Strelecki
Senior Editor/Group Manager: Vicki Leigh Ingham
Senior Associate Design Director: Ken Carlson

Publisher and Editor in Chief: James D. Blume
Editorial Director: Linda Raglan Cunningham
Executive Director, Marketing: Jeffrey B. Myers
Executive Director, New Business Development: Todd M. Davis
Executive Director, Sales: Ken Zagor
Director, Operations: George A. Susral
Director, Production: Douglas M. Johnston
Business Director: Jim Leonard

Vice President and General Manager: Douglas J. Guendel

***Better Homes and Gardens®* Magazine**
Editor in Chief: Karol DeWulf Nickell
Deputy Editor, Home Design: Oma Blaise Ford

Meredith Publishing Group
President: Jack Griffin
Senior Vice President: Bob Mate

Meredith Corporation
Chairman and Chief Executive Officer: William T. Kerr
President and Chief Operating Officer: Stephen M. Lacy

In Memoriam: E.T. Meredith III (1933-2003)

Copyright © 2005 by Meredith Corporation, Des Moines, Iowa. First Edition.
All rights reserved. Printed in the United States of America.
Library of Congress Control Number: 2004115506
ISBN: 0-696-22551-4

All of us at Meredith® Books are dedicated to providing you with information and ideas to enhance your home. We welcome your comments and suggestions. Write to us at: Meredith Books, Home Decorating and Design Editorial Department, 1716 Locust St., Des Moines, IA 50309-3023.

If you would like to purchase any of our home decorating and design, cooking, crafts, gardening, or home improvement books, check wherever quality books are sold. Or visit us at: bhgbooks.com

If you're like most parents, you're interested in creating comfortable, inviting rooms for your kids—without blowing your budget.

That's where this book comes in.

You'll discover great decorating ideas—whether your child is a baby, grade-schooler, or teen—and each one is under $50.

So let your creativity flow. Create curtain tiebacks out of baby shoes from the dollar store. Design a low-cost sports-themed room for a kid who lives for hockey. Fashion an inexpensive wooden headboard for a teen who loves nature.

Then add those fun little touches that make a room special—for only a few bucks. Use a cute bandanna window treatment to set a Western mood. Create a shimmering iced candle to delight teens who are into romance. Display antique doll bonnets to create charm in a nursery.

You'll even find tips on how to involve your kids in decorating—and how it can teach them important lessons on budgeting. So when your guests comment on your new decor, you and your kids can proudly say, "Thanks, we did it together."

6 babies

From great ways to spruce up secondhand furniture to creating a thrifty circus canopy, you'll discover ideas to make your nursery cozy and charming. Plus you'll find out how to beautify rooms with borders and add sparkle with garage-sale finds.

20 kids

Here are the ingredients you'll need to create lively rooms for grade-schoolers. From original wall art to awesome accessories, each idea costs less than $50.

44 teens

Got a teenager who loves gardening … fishing … slumber parties? Choose an inexpensive decorating theme to match your teen's personality and favorite hobbies.

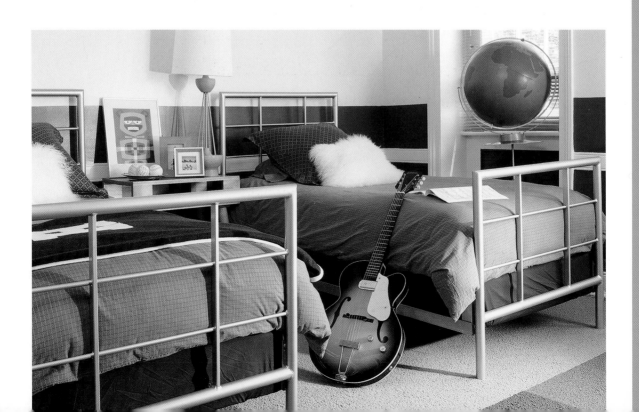

68 windows

Come explore exciting window treatments that cost less than you'd imagine. Learn how to add pizzazz with vibrant valances, romantic gauze, and fun tiebacks.

88 paint

Paint costs little yet contributes a lot, letting you create all kinds of looks, from a dinosaur headboard to a deep blue sea. Here you'll find how to choose the colors and tools that will help you achieve professional results.

104 accents

You'll love these affordable ideas for eye-catching accessories. From a wagon bedside table to colorful patchwork lampshades and rehabbed outdoor furniture—these innovative ideas are easy on the wallet.

It's natural to want everything to match and work together in your baby's nursery; you want the room to be as perfect as your new arrival. So how do you begin? First remember that the whole world is fresh for your baby, including used furniture and secondhand furnishings. Knowing this will help you stay within your budget and have fun decorating.

save with secondhand

To indulge your decorating urges while sticking to your budget, begin with pre-owned furniture. Good pieces for less than $50 sometimes show up at garage sales, The Salvation Army, Disabled American Veterans' (DAV) stores, thrift shops, and auctions. A little sanding and some colorful paint can transform an ordinary piece, giving it great style at almost half the cost of new furniture.

Begin by choosing pieces appropriate for any age (some cribs will convert to toddler beds and daybeds); then use baby accessories to create your nursery. Add the same stencil design to all the pieces and they'll look as if you bought them as a set.

how to
choose a safe used crib

Before purchasing a crib for your baby, take some safety precautions, especially if you're buying it secondhand.

1 Check that the slats or posts are no more than 2 inches apart. If the spaces are wider than that, part of your newborn's body might slip through and be injured.
2 The space between the mattress and all four sides of the crib should be no wider than two adult fingers.
3 Avoid decorative cutouts that could trap a baby's head or limbs.
4 If the crib is painted, check the paint for lead content. Any amount of lead is unacceptable, because a baby may chew on the crib when teething and ingest the harmful substance.

pick a theme

Choose a theme to help guide you as you begin to furnish and decorate your nursery. It could be a character theme—or something as simple as two coordinating colors. One popular look is a cloud motif, created by painting a room sky blue and sponge-painting clouds near the ceiling. Or create a jungle theme with painted trees and grasses on the walls and accessorize with stuffed baby jungle animals from garage sales or consignment shops.

PAINT POWER A used four-poster crib, *opposite*, takes on a whole new personality when the ends and sides are painted different pastel colors.

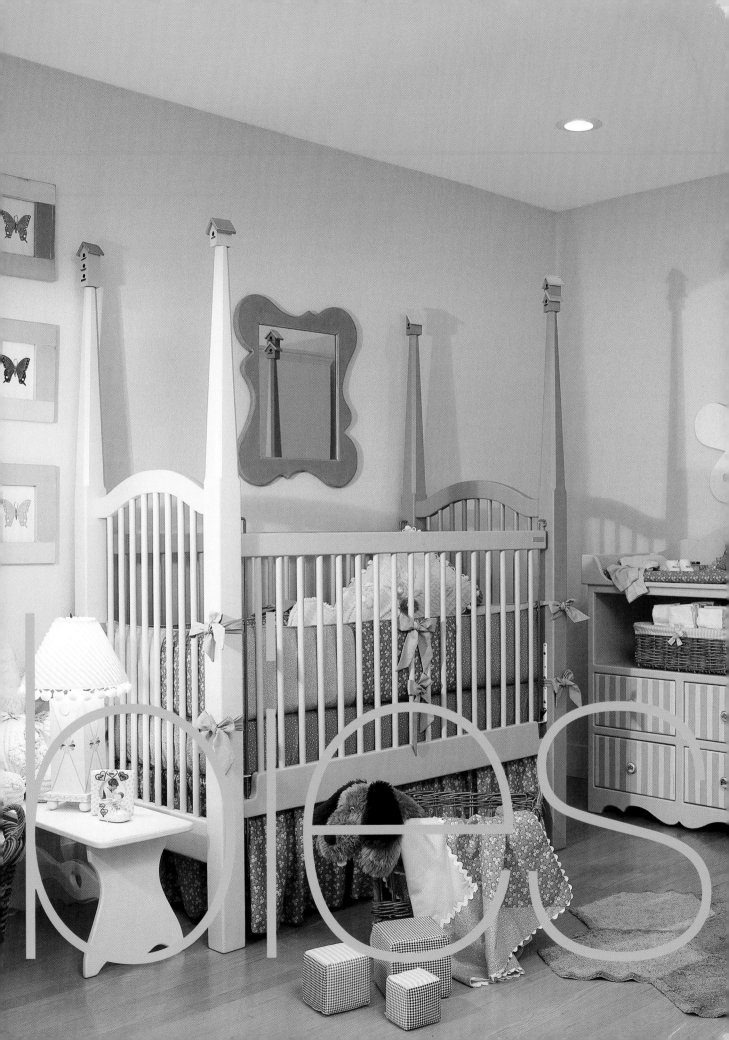

go bold and beautiful

Paint can offer a lot of change for little money. To maximize the bargain, check your neighborhood paint store for paints that have been discontinued. You may pick up paint for as little as $5 per gallon or $1 per quart. If you stop by often, you could find a color you love.

Create a room full of fantasy and fun by adding the element of color. A vivid canopy in a bold array of gender-neutral colors will turn your baby's room into a happy haven and provide the visual stimulation that's essential for your newborn.

It's easy to change the environment of the room using paint, paper, or large posters. A vast selection of nursery wallpaper is available today, much of it at discount department stores. Paint is also affordable and makes a redo fast when your baby turns toddler.

UNDER THE BIG TOP An eye-catching mobile, *below* ($8–$18 at home discount stores), or canopy, *opposite,* helps provide the motion and color necessary for a baby's developing eyes.

sew this circus canopy

Materials and Tools

Measuring tape
54-inch-wide fabric
Backing and low-loft quilt batting
Thread and pins
Sewing machine

Scissors
4 cup hooks
2 narrow metal curtain rods
Small stuffed animals

1 To determine the length of 54-inch-wide fabric you'll need to measure the wall from the top of the baseboard to the ceiling. Add 60 inches for the canopy. Allow the same amount for the backing and batting and 2 additional yards for the binding (based on a 54×30-inch crib).
2 Sandwich low-loft quilt batting between two layers of fabric, right sides facing out. Baste or pin the layers together. Sew through all three layers at 3-inch intervals or along design lines.
3 Cut one end to create the pointed edges as seen in the photograph *opposite*. Bind all sides with 1-inch-wide strips cut on the cross grain.
4 Using cup hooks, hang one narrow metal curtain rod where the ceiling and wall meet. Hang another rod parallel to that and 30 inches out from the first rod. Check that the rods fit securely into the hooks.
5 Drape the canopy along the wall and over both rods. Adjust the canopy to swag as shown. Sew stuffed animals to the points.

create a canopy for less than $50

Choosing sophisticated fabrics—those that can shift with the times as your child matures—is a smart long-term investment. Selecting colors with staying power (here peach with rosy accents) will keep the look fresh well into the teen years. The mounted ruffled canopy, *left,* a classic decorating idea, can serve as a headboard for a preschooler or preteen, thanks to a carefully chosen fabric.

The result? A pastel palette of plaids, checks, and florals that will add lasting charm for your little one for years to come.

To stretch your budget, check fabric store sale tables, where bolts of discontinued fabrics may be as much as 60 percent off. Or use a queen- or king-size flat sheet—which costs as little as $20 at a home discount center or $5 at a neighborhood garage sale.

Add a timeless club chair and ottoman dressed in matching ruffled skirts, frothy balloon shades, a floral needlepoint rug, and an array of printed throw pillows—as shown, *opposite*—to complete the cozy look.

 **how to**

make this peach canopy (for experienced sewers)

Materials and Tools

$3/_4$-inch plywood
Wood glue
Paper
2 pairs of L-brackets
54-inch-wide fabric to size
  (see below)

Sewing machine
Equal yardage lining fabric
Thread and pins
Pearl cotton
Staple gun and staples

1 Use two layers of plywood glued together for a circular form. To make the pattern, draw a 24×32-inch oval on paper. Cut it in half, leaving a 24×16$^1/_2$-inch shape. Fit the flat side of the plywood to the wall, 7$^1/_2$ inches from ceiling, and support it with L-brackets secured to the studs.

2 Cut and piece fabric to make two panels, each ceiling to floor in length and 50 inches wide. Taper the panels so the center hangs 12 inches off the floor and the outer edge touches the floor. Cut the lining pieces to match. Finish the inner edges with a 3-inch ruffle and piping. Sew the lining to the curtain, right sides together, leaving an opening. Turn, press, and sew closed. Gather the edges around the form; tack.

3 For the valance, cut and piece a panel 25 inches deep and 6 yards wide. Finish the lower and short ends with ruffle and piping, curving the shape at corners. Turn under the upper edge 3 inches for the ruffle; stitch.

4 Starting at the base of the top ruffle, mark 15 to 20 rows for smocking; space rows $^1/_2$ inches apart. Lay a piece of pearl cotton along the marked line; pin. Leave a 6-inch tail at each end. Using a wide zigzag stitch, sew over the pearl cotton. Don't catch the cotton in the stitch. Repeat for the remaining rows.

5 Starting at one end, pull all pearl cotton ends and gather them to the center of the panel. Start at the other end and gather the remainder of the panel. Pull gathers to fit the form; overlap the ends. Anchor the pearl cotton with machine stitches. Staple the valance to the form. Adjust the gathers to cover the staples. Hang the form on the wall.

6 Sew two lined fabric bows. Pull the curtains back with the bows. Tie the curtains to wall-mounted hooks.

beautify with borders for less

From top to bottom, your baby's nursery needs to be comfortable; yet it should be ready for change as your child grows up. Though wallpaper border may appear permanent, it's actually easy to remove. Borders are available in a great number of designs, ranging from ABCs to colorful storybook characters such as Alice in Wonderland and the Three Bears.

Borders are a high-impact, low-cost decorating move. What's more, they're as easy to install as they are to eliminate, so they'll also save you time when you redo the room.

For added interest and charm, consider stenciling designs that match the border onto dressers and other furnishings.

BORDER MAGIC If a ceiling seems too high, use an extra-wide border to visually lower it and create a sense of intimacy, *opposite*. Borders are $30–$45 for an average-size nursery. You'll save even more if you look for discontinued styles.

BASIC BLUE A painted border can also be effective. The deep blue border in the room, *below*, contrasts with the crisp white walls for a fresh, inviting look.

how to
hang border wallpaper

Hanging wallpaper borders is an easy, affordable way to add charm to your nursery. Follow these steps and your border will be up in a snap. HINT: It's even quicker with a partner, so ask a friend to help and then repay the favor in kind.

Materials and Tools

Prepasted wallpaper border

Vinyl-to-vinyl adhesive (if you're installing the border over wallpaper)

Wallpaper brush

Cloth

1 Purchase a prepasted border. Immerse the loosely rolled border in water and slowly pull it out, taking care not to crease it and checking that both the front and back are completely wet.

2 If you prefer not to use water to activate the prepaste adhesive, new prepaste activators are easy to apply. Use a roller to apply the activator to your border. If you're installing the border over wallpaper, use vinyl-to-vinyl adhesive.

3 Start in the least conspicuous corner when you begin putting up the border (that way if you don't end up with a perfect match in pattern when the ends connect, it won't be noticeable).

4 Use a wallpaper brush to remove any creases or air bubbles and adhere the border to the wall. Use a damp cloth to wipe off any excess paste that oozes out from the edges.

THRIFTY TODDLER TRANSFORMATION
Changing a nursery, *opposite,* into a toddler's room, *above,* can be quick and inexpensive: Replace the tiny rocker with a larger chair, take down the front crib railing, and add a blue footstool for easy climbing into bed.

NEAT SHEETS Transform ordinary flat sheets into fabric yardage to make window treatments, pillows, or bed skirts, *above,* for less than $10 per sheet.

 to

make a duvet cover and curtains from sheets

Making curtains and other accessories out of bedsheets guarantees easy care and affordability. If you shop at white sales in your local department stores, you may bag an even better bargain. Here's how to use the yardage:

Materials and Tools

Flat sheets	Thread	Curtain rods
Sewing machine	Snaps	

1 Use flat sheets to make a duvet cover. Buy two flat sheets to fit the bed, seam them on three sides, and add snaps to the fourth side. Slip your comforter inside for an instant makeover.

2 Buy a full-size flat sheet to make curtains. Hem one end to length; then make a pocket hem at the top to house your curtain rod.

use unisex colors

More than a patriotic theme, the color scheme, *below,* offers a gender-neutral solution if you're eager to decorate but don't know your baby's sex. Red, white, and blue colors are also strong enough to provide the visual variety your baby needs. Keep your primary colors in check by adding plenty of neutral white in your furnishings. This helps provide relief from the powerful punch of strong color.

Or add a few yellow accents and the primary palette is complete. Classic pairs such as blue and yellow or blue and green make a good base for a nursery that's neither feminine nor masculine. When it's time to change the room, keep one color and pair it with another for a fresh look.

Nautical, fishing, and Americana motifs are examples of themes using primary colors that withstand the test of time. Add small, easily changeable framed prints, throw pillows, or rugs for thrifty updates as your child grows.

hot tip

To find cheap fabrics, look for outlet stores in your town or check under "fabrics" in the Yellow Pages. You'll probably find fabrics discounted as much as 50 to 90 percent.

CUDDLE TIME Add a few cute decorating throw pillows ($6–$8 at home discount stores), garage sale stuffed animals ($1–$3 each), and a new cover ($25) to an easy chair to create a spot that's perfect for naptime storytelling.

repurpose what you have

Every nursery needs a big, comfy chair for cuddling. If you have one that fits the bill, introduce it to the room and help it fit in by sewing a new cover out of sheets that coordinate with your nursery theme.

Better yet, go with a no-sew option: Tuck the sheets carefully under the cushions and pin them to the back with decorator tacks in matching colors.

If you don't have a chair on hand that will work, look for cozy stuffed chairs at secondhand stores or garage sales. Those with worn coverings sell for $30 or less. Re-cover the chair with a quilt or tablecloth in hues that harmonize with the color scheme to give it a new look.

If you have Internet access, surf these websites for deals on baby furniture and accessories:
ababy.com
babybargainsusa.com
babystore.indiaserver.com/baby-
    furniture.html
babymajesty.com
bizrate.com
greatstartpage.com
shopping.com

protect your baby at home

1 Get down on your hands and knees and look at everything from your new arrival's viewpoint.
2 Be on the lookout for small or sharp items. Most babies will put anything they find into their mouths. Keep surfaces clear of paper clips, coins, cigarettes, and other small objects. Put scissors, knives, and razor blades out of reach.
3 Cover unused electrical outlets with plastic plugs (available at hardware stores). Keep lamp cords out of the way behind the furniture.
4 Move all cleaning supplies and medicine into a locked cabinet. Never tell your baby that medicine is "candy."
5 Beware of hot food. Always test the temperature of food or liquids warmed up in a microwave oven, because some heat unevenly.
6 Put away all plastic bags, especially ones that cover dry-cleaned items.
7 Install safety gates at the top and bottom of open stairways.
8 Learn cardiopulmonary resuscitation (CPR) and the Heimlich maneuver (for dislodging food or a foreign object that is choking someone) and install a fire detector.

HOT POCKETS Handy hanging pockets are perfect for holding your baby's rattles, toys, and stuffed animals. Buy or create this fun storage solution for less than $25.

try low-cost clutter cutters

Organizing your baby's books, clothes, and toys can be a daunting task as gifts come rolling in. Forget expensive toy chests, where items often get mangled or broken.

Instead use inexpensive plastic storage bins with lids—$5–$12 at discount department stores—to sort everything: one bin for books, one for animals, another for dress-up costumes, and so on.

Choose containers that are appropriate for the size of the items in each category. Plastic bins stack effortlessly in a closet or in a corner or can slide under the bed. If you want something a little more stylish, cover shoeboxes with wallpaper, fabric, or even wrapping paper, using colors that fit the nursery scheme.

If you don't like boxes or bins, consider hanging storage. Wall pockets (similar to a plastic shoe bag with rows of shoe compartments) made from fabric or painter's canvas will hold many different items. Or use a peg rack ($1 at dollar stores or $10–12 for sturdier ones at home discount centers) to hang the wall pockets. When your child ages, the peg rack can hold caps, jackets, and older kids' items.

Here are other thrifty, easy solutions for organizing small items:

- **Store jigsaw puzzles in freezer bags** ($1 for 20 at dollar stores).
- **Use stackable plastic milk crates** ($5–$6 each) to hold cars and other toys.
- **Hang a small hammock** ($8–$10) from bedposts for stuffed animals.
- **Stash secret treasures** (those odds and ends found in the park or on the beach) in old cookie tins (a couple of dollars each at garage sales or Goodwill stores).
- **Construct rustic storage** from packing crates (often free at grocery stores). Sand the surface to eliminate splinters and remove any staples. The open shelves can display family and baby photos.

Pockets stitched to a bed skirt, *below,* are perfect for storing bedtime books and favorite stuffed animals—still handy, yet off the floor. They're a low-cost touch that can help coordinate the bed with the overall decorating scheme.

Kids grow up so fast. So when decorating their bedrooms, you have to be creative in your decor and your budget to keep up with their changing tastes. Choose basic furnishings, fabrics, and accessories that can adapt as your child grows, and you'll stretch your budget.

For delightful accents, turn to flea market or garage sale finds and refurbish them for a few dollars. In this chapter you'll discover thrifty headboards, wall art, and decorating themes that will transform your child's room into a special, personalized space.

For floors in kids' rooms, choose stain- and wear-resistant coverings that can handle spills and crayon marks. In high-traffic areas consider topping permanent coverings with low-cost, washable throw rugs that come with a nonskid backing.

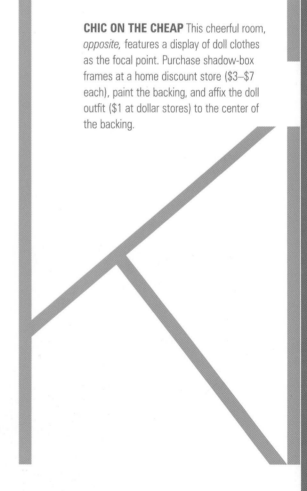

CHIC ON THE CHEAP This cheerful room, *opposite*, features a display of doll clothes as the focal point. Purchase shadow-box frames at a home discount store ($3–$7 each), paint the backing, and affix the doll outfit ($1 at dollar stores) to the center of the backing.

decorate around a mural

Check local stores
for inexpensive
murals or search
online. Websites
with a good
selection are:
usawallpaper.com and
berlinwallpaper.com.

A wall mural is a low-cost way to spruce up a kid's room. You'll have fun choosing from numerous scenes, from baby animals and fairy tales to racing cars and views of outer space. Wall murals can open up your room while creating a three-dimensional visual effect that paint alone usually isn't able to accomplish.

Most murals consist of two to eight panels and are easy to hang in a couple of hours. They can be applied to a painted surface or over existing wallpaper.

To narrow down your choices, look for a mural based on your child's favorite color. Then add white, off-white, and one or two accent colors that harmonize with the furnishings. To create a monochromatic room instead, focus on one shade of the favorite color and add slight variations as accents.

Colors can be classified as either warm or cool. If the color has yellow undertones, it's warm: orange, fire-engine red, yellow-green. If it has blue undertones, it's cool: royal blue, maroon, and deep forest green.

Here's one way to classify colors:
- **Warm Colors** (Red, Pink, Orange, Yellow): These active colors seem to move forward, communicating vigor, cheer, and excitement. They stimulate the appetite and evoke emotions.
- **Cool Colors** (Green, Blue, Purple): These passive colors recede into the background, cool you down, calm your nerves, and promote introspection.
- **Neutral Colors** (Brown, Beige, Taupe, Gray, Black, White): These colors are easy on the eyes, symbolize a down-to-earth attitude, make you feel secure, and work well with other colors.

ROOM TO GROW A garden mural, *opposite*, adds a fanciful touch to this youngster's room. Wallpaper offers an easy alternative to hand-painted murals if you're not particularly artistic. Most wallpaper murals are $16–$49. Add thrifty accents such as artificial flowers from the local thrift shop (only $2–$10).

hang a mural

Most murals come in easy-to-handle panels that you put together like a puzzle. Follow the manufacturer's instructions for installation. If instructions are unavailable, follow these general rules:

Materials and Tools

Wallpaper paste (if needed)	Straightedge ruler
Pencil	Sponge
Wallpaper brush	

1 Mix the paste (before purchasing a mural ask whether the paste is included).
2 Mark the wall with vertical and horizontal lines with a pencil.
3 Apply the paste to the backside of the panels.
4 Position the panels top to bottom.
5 Smooth the panels with a wallpaper brush.
6 Use a straightedge ruler to trim the paper to the exact dimension.
7 Wipe the panels with a damp sponge to remove excess paste.

get wall art for less

Wall art can wow without emptying your wallet. What children want to display on their bedroom walls says a lot about their personalities, so let them make a statement. Hobbies, sports, and fantasies all play a part in defining who they are.

When children outgrow what they have on their walls, let them have some fun in the makeover process. Encourage them to create inexpensive handmade projects that they can scatter throughout the room. Keep things simple, lighthearted, and fun, and you'll be amazed at the results.

THE ONE THAT GOT AWAY An oar, $15–$25 at stores that sell used sporting goods, sets an active mood, *above*. A colorful headboard and a painted lamp help finish the look.

DRESS IT UP Art can go frameless. These quaint vintage outfits, *opposite*, add charm to an old corner wardrobe. If you don't have any that are suitable for display, find them for about $10–$25 each at flea markets or antique shops.

how to

create thrifty art for kids' rooms

1. Install a plain painted shelf (about $15 at home stores, $2 for spray paint) above a door, window, or closet and fill it with favorite collectibles and toys.
2. Refresh a rustic garden gate ($15–$35 at garage sales or thrift shops) with new color, hang it on the wall above a desk, and use it to display colorful school art projects.
3. Make handprints of each family member. Have each person put one hand in paint and press the hand on a ceramic tile. Then paint the person's name below the print and hang the tile on the wall. Suspend the tiles from cup hooks, using vibrant ribbons that match the decor of the room. The cost is $3 per tile, $3 for cup hooks, and $4 for ribbon.
4. If your child is into sports, hang used sports equipment on the walls; skateboards, hockey sticks, ice skates, baseball gloves, or football helmets. You'll probably be able to gather a variety at tag sales or thrift shops for under $25.
5. For a vintage-style room, old tin ceiling tiles ($10–$35 at salvage yards) spray-painted in varying colors and lined across a wall add a nostalgic touch.
6. A display of current and vintage hats and bonnets ($3–$15 each at antique and discount clothing stores) can add colorful flair to a plain wall.

hot tip

Invest your decorating dollars with long-term growth in mind: Plan and design hardworking rooms that can grow and adapt with your child. Whether you have a newborn, a school-age child, or both, avoid age-specific products and motifs that will require replacement in just a year or two.

do a quick change

It inevitably happens: The little girl or boy who once wanted to be cuddled in your arms begins to grow up. It's important for school-age kids to have a place to call their own, and that place is usually their bedroom.

When your child transitions from bunnies to skateboards or lullabies to soccer, it's time for a bedroom makeover. If you chose versatile, timeless pieces for the nursery, your job will be easy, because you can give that furniture a quick makeover with paint.

PAST TO PRESENT The new wallpaper, *below*, easily complements furniture once used in the nursery. Low-cost white tulle ($2–$10 per yard) and floral swags ($3–$10 at home discount centers) make great bed canopies.

HAPPY TRAILS Low-cost Western items add character, *opposite*. A simple footstool is re-covered in faux cowhide ($15–$30 for the footstool at secondhand stores and $3 per yard for faux hide). A wooden armoire once filled with baby clothes dons decoupaged cowboy prints. Western accessories tie the whole look together.

incorporate
their likes

Whether your child is 2 or 12, you can use his or her hobbies or interests as a theme for decorating the room. Low-cost accessories such as window valances, toys, and wall art can carry the theme and help you achieve a custom look without a large price tag.

Take some time with your child to brainstorm. Together imagine what the completed room could look like. Make a list of wants and needs and, if possible, make the final decisions as a team.

BACK AT THE RANCH This sturdy furniture, *opposite,* recalls an old bunkhouse. Get accent items such as cowboy hats and Western prints ($1–$10 each) at thrift shops. If you sew, buy material with a Western theme and add color-coordinated fringed trim for window valances.

PRIMARILY SIMPLE Primary colors and familiar cartoon characters, *below,* appeal to many children. Bunk beds can be rearranged or repainted to suit changing needs. Stuffed animals may be found at garage sales ($1–$5).

hot tip

Most school-age children enjoy participating in some decorating decisions. Ask them how their favorite colors, hobbies, or sports can be used in the theme. Bring home fabric samples and let them choose their favorites.

A THREE-ALARM ROOM The bed, *above,* is custom-built; the theme it portrays can be adapted for a modest budget. Paint a used ladder ($8–$20 at thrift shops) red and mount it over a headboard painted yellow. Inexpensive toy fire engines are plentiful at garage sales. Look for stuffed-animal Dalmatians to add authenticity.

building on a theme

To pull off a good decorating scheme in your child's room, limit the number of patterned fabrics to three or four. Use white or other neutral colors to cool down bright tones. Let your child pick a favorite fabric, painting, or print as the beginning feature and then add coordinating basics. Add the motif to a variety of surfaces, from walls and windows to bedspreads and lampshades.

For an elementary-age child, choose furniture that's classic enough to suit future needs and decorating schemes. Add color by painting bedposts or installing new hardware on dressers and side tables. Consider the following ideas and then let your imagination take over.

If you have a budding ballerina in your family, keep a collection of outgrown ballet slippers or tap shoes. Hang the slippers from pretty ribbons on decorative hooks along the wall or use them as tiebacks for curtains. Or display used tap shoes in a shadow box.

Outgrown tutus or leotards can dress a favorite stuffed bear or two, arranged on the bed. Display black and white photographs from dance recitals on the wall or on a dresser to recall pleasant memories.

Purchase a durable plastic playground slide or teeter-totter at a garage sale ($20–$30). They will fit into a child's room quite easily and will give kids hours of fun. Stencil a hopscotch pattern on an inexpensive solid-color throw rug and tack the rug to the floor. Purchase or sew small beanbags in fun fabrics to toss on each number as the game is played.

AROUND THE WORLD If your child likes maps or travel, plan an expedition to the thrift shop and hunt for old globes ($2–$15). Displayed as a group, *above,* they'll have extra impact.

get sporty—for less

If your child or teen loves sports, add a bench for putting on shoes; you may find a bargain in the classified newspaper or neighborhood shopper ads or on the Web. Hang a team T-shirt or jersey above the headboard (or even in place of a headboard) in tribute to your child's favorite sport or sports figure.

Used baseballs and small sports-action figures are perfect accessories for a sports theme. You may be able to find these for $1–$10 each at garage sales.

Or display an artistic poster of a sports star, *above*. Such posters are available for $12–$15 at allposters.com. To make a poster the focal point of the room, order a standard size and frame it.

ALL IN THE GAME Inexpensive ($8–$12) metal folding chairs, *above*, can be spray-painted to match your color scheme. They make great seating at a desk or study table.

hot tip

Crafts stores sell wood letters ready for painting—these make fun room additions. Let your child spell out a word or phrase that expresses his or her individuality.

HOME RUN Give wood bifold closet doors, *below,* the championship treatment with paint and padlocks (at sporting-goods stores for $3–$6). Put small sports pictures in inexpensive frames ($8–$15 each) to serve as wall art. Or attach unframed pictures to the wall with hook-and-loop tape.

wow 'em with wallpaper

For easy transformations select wallpaper that supports the color scheme and fits the scale of the room. Consider whether the pattern will have lasting appeal. Cartoon-themed wallpaper, a common choice, can go out of style very quickly.

On the average a child's room measures 10×12 feet. In small rooms a modest pattern will give walls character and appeal without compromising the illusion of space. Larger rooms can handle more energetic prints if the prints coordinate with accessories.

To make the best choice, pick out several wallpaper patterns, allow your child to choose favorites, and then make the final decision together.

BLUE BEAUTY A small wallpaper pattern, *below,* yields to boldly painted furnishings and harmonizes with the color scheme. A flea-market lamp ($5–$10), along with frames ($1–$5), adds character.

MIX AND MATCH Florals, plaids, and simple stripes mix freely, *opposite*. To avoid clashes choose patterns of different sizes and use color as a unifying factor. Limit the number of patterns to three or four.

calculate wallpaper needs

Tools
Measuring tape   Calculator

1 Measure the square footage of the walls by multiplying the wall height by the total wall width. Divide the result by the square footage of one single roll of your chosen wallcovering (coverage amounts differ depending on paper selection) to find out how many rolls you'll need.

2 Wallcoverings are calculated in single rolls but often are sold in double rolls (also called bolts). Divide the amount of wallcovering you need by 2 if you buy double rolls.

3 When measuring don't deduct for openings such as doors, windows, or built-in shelving. This will allow for pattern matching, trimming, and waste.

4 Consider ordering an extra roll for mistakes or later repairs and keep a record of the pattern name and number and dye-lot number in case you have to reorder. Always ask a store associate to double-check your roll calculations before ordering.

hot tip

If necessary, old wallpaper can be left in place and covered with a new layer. Cover the old paper with wallpaper primer to hide the pattern and to provide a good bonding surface. Position the new seams carefully so they do not line up with the old ones.

how to
remove old wallpaper

Materials and Tools

Drop cloths	Wallpaper scoring tool
Wallpaper stripper	Sponge
Wallpaper scraping tool	

1 Protect baseboards and floors with drop cloths to catch stripper drips and wallpaper scraps.
2 Work a corner of the wallcovering loose and pull it carefully. If the wallcovering pulls away some of the wall surface, use wallpaper stripper in liquid or gel form to loosen the paper. Gels tend to be less messy than liquids and soak into the paper better. After you've applied the wallpaper stripper, remove the paper with a wallpaper scraping tool.
3 If the wallpaper doesn't loosen, the stripper hasn't penetrated the surface. Score the wallpaper carefully with a wallpaper scoring tool.
4 Reapply the stripper and continue scraping until all the paper is removed.
5 Using a damp cloth or sponge, clean any remaining residue off the wall and let the surface dry.

MAKING HAY The old hay feeder, *above,* purchased for a few dollars at a farm auction, can hold magazines and books to help keep your kids' clutter at bay.

FLEA-MARKET DESK The roomy desk, *opposite,* was too rough to write on, so the owners covered the top with an old school map and a piece of custom-cut glass to create a one-of-a-kind workstation for under $50.

bargain-hunt together

If you're serious about cutting expenses, decorate your child's room with items you already have. Look in your garage or basement, and you may find an object or two to inspire you.

For example, an older sibling may no longer want outdated framed posters or pictures. For no-cost artwork let your youngsters create their own wall art with finger paints or chalk in a coordinating palette of colors.

If you have a grade-schooler, start a collection together. Whether you're looking for old china teacups or used baseballs ($2–$8) you can use the results to decorate the room. Peruse garage sales and flea markets to search for these items. Your child may want to pass them on to his or her children. An economical purchase may become an heirloom.

If you have even a tiny budget, make your search for low-cost decorating items a fun family affair. Set a date with your kids to visit consignment shops, "scratch-and-dent" furniture sales, or your local thrift store.

"mark it mine" —for pennies

If your kids would enjoy creating their own masterpieces, consider installing a wall-art center for older children or preteens. It's inexpensive, and a great way to encourage their creativity, whether they want to draw, paint, or write poems or stories.

The art center can be mounted (and remounted) to suit the size of your kids, and the "blank canvas" it provides is big enough to accommodate a mural if that's what they choose to paint.

THE WRITING IS ON THE WALL Hang rolls of paper on a wooden drapery rod (under $25 at large retail stores) supported by brackets. Or mount a huge pad of paper on the wall for kids to draw on (about $12 at most office supply stores).

create a wall-art center

Materials

Heavy-duty brackets
Wooden drapery rod

Large roll of brown kraft paper or white paper

1 Hang brackets at a desirable height that your kids can reach and far enough apart to accommodate the roll of paper.
2 Insert the roll of paper on a wooden drapery rod and hang the rod on the brackets.
3 Roll the paper down to the floor and turn your kids loose with crayons or markers in a rainbow of colors.
4 To change the paper, extend the used "page" plus a few inches of unused paper across the floor. Fold the paper back, matching the sides and making a crease. Cut along the crease and roll the clean paper back up off the floor.

Here are a few websites that offer some products that may inspire you with ideas for reviving an old headboard:

bhg.com

potterybarnkids.com

nextag.com

readysethome.com

hearthsong.com

how to

create a baseball headboard

Materials and Tools

Jigsaw
Plywood cut to fit (see below)
Measuring tape
Pencil
Sandpaper

Hammer and nails
Latex or acrylic paint: white, brown, and
　　other desired colors
Paintbrushes
Fine artist's brush for detailing

1 For ball-and-bat sides, cut two 1×6-inch plywood pieces 55 inches long. Draw a 5-inch-diameter ball at one end of each piece, centering the ball across the width of the board.

2 Referring to the photograph, *above,* draw an outline of a bat. Cut four 1×6-inch wood pieces 50 inches long for pickets. (You'll need to cut six or seven for a full-size bed, depending on spacing.)

3 Cut a point at one end of each picket or look at a lumber store for precut pickets in the size you need. Smooth rough edges with sandpaper.

4 Cut two 1×3-inch boards the same width as the bed frame. Lay these supports 12 inches apart on a flat surface.

5 Position the ball-and-bat pieces on each end of the support boards and put the pickets in between them along the supports; nail in place. Paint the bats and pickets in desired colors.

6 Paint the balls white, adding brown stitching with a fine artist's paintbrush.

design a thrifty headboard

Whether your kid's tastes are simple or elaborate, a headboard is the perfect way to reflect his or her personality. Get together with your child for a brainstorming session and let the creative juices flow as you design a backdrop for the bed.

A new twin-size headboard ranges from $100 to $300 for solid wood and from $75 to $150 for metal. So start with a headboard you have or purchase one at a garage sale or flea market for less than $50. And remember, a headboard alone will do; a footboard is optional and will cost more.

Hide imperfections with a little paint, fabric, and maybe some stenciling or freehand floral designs. You'll save money, and by working together, you'll create a bonding experience.

PLAY BALL The easy-to-make, economical headboard, *opposite,* is sure to be a hit with any major-league boy or girl. The lumber ($30), nails ($5), and paintbrushes ($2) can be purchased at home building centers.

GARDEN-FRESH The simple fence headboard, *below,* is made of stockade fencing ($30 at home building stores). Add the sandpaper ($2), latex primer ($6), paint ($8), and drywall screws ($3), and the project is still under $50. For stability anchor the fence to the wall instead of the bed.

make a picket-fence headboard

Materials and Tools

Measuring tape	Latex primer and paint in desired colors
Reassembled stockade fencing	Paintbrushes
Jigsaw (optional)	Drywall screws, anchor bolts,
Sandpaper	or other fasteners
Tack cloth	Screwdriver

1 Measure the width of the bed and decide how high you want the top of the headboard to be. Have the fencing cut to size or cut it yourself.
2 Sand surfaces and wipe them with a tack cloth. Prime and paint the fencing.
3 Stand the fencing in place. Using drywall screws, anchor bolts, or other appropriate fasteners, attach the fence to the wall at several points on each side. Slide the bed against the fence.
4 For a bed that sits diagonally across a corner, you may need to cut triangular blocks of scrap wood 1×2 inches or 2×4 inches for braces. Attach the blocks to the wall; then attach the fence to the blocks. Use several blocks on each side to ensure stability.

transform with hardware

hot tip

Not sure where to
find an assortment
of knobs and pulls?
Check your local
hardware store,
retail home centers,
or one of the
websites which
offer a number
of choices:

coolknobsandpulls.com

vandykes.com

goknobs.com

Who would have thought you could transform the look of an entire room with only a few pieces of hardware? A change of drawer pulls and knobs can make a dramatic difference, taking furniture from drab to fab.

If you're going to refinish a piece of furniture and change the hardware, plan your color scheme first. When searching for that right pull or knob, take the paint chips you've selected with you. This will make it easier to envision the completed project.

A once-boring dresser or nightstand, *right and opposite,* takes on new life with a fresh coat of paint and pretty pulls. White-washing and sanding the edges will give your piece a vintage look. Or go bold with sponge-painting and ceramic flower handles.

The average cost for basic pulls and knobs is $1–$5 each. Save more by shopping local crafts stores and home centers, which carry a variety of plain wooden knobs and pulls that may be painted or embellished.

For example, if you have a seaside bedroom theme, choose simple wooden knobs that may be painted then glue on seashells or colorful fish.

MARVELOUS MAKEOVERS A soft color palette, *above and opposite,* on secondhand furniture creates a youthful mood. A change of color and updated hardware (about $25) on the vanity create a thrifty makeover. Hand-painted wooden knobs on the dresser, *below,* add color and interest.

how to

create decorative wooden knobs

Materials and Tools

Plain wooden knobs	Paintbrush
Sandpaper	Colored pencil
Primer	Stencils (optional)
Latex or acrylic paint	Small artist's or stenciling brush
in desired colors	Polyurethane

1 Purchase plain wooden knobs that fit on the same screws as the existing ones.

2 Sand, clean, and prime the knobs; let dry.

3 Paint the knobs with a base coat of latex or acrylic paint in the desired colors.

4 Paint a design on the knob. A simple design is best for small surfaces; consider a floral, fruit, star, or polka-dot design. If you're painting freehand, practice drawing your design on a piece of paper. When you're satisfied with your picture, use a colored pencil to duplicate the design on the knob. If you prefer to stencil the design, either purchase ready-made stencils or make your own with clear acetate sheets.

5 After you transfer the drawing to the knob or put the stencil in place, paint the design in latex or acrylic colors with a small artist's or stenciling brush. Seal with two coats of polyurethane.

Decorating with teens can be a blast. Often they're open to new and unusual ideas and will be thrilled to know you want to design a space especially for them. Would your teen like a boudoir with a Parisian twist, a retro look, or a gardener's retreat? You'll discover these and other original ideas for teens' bedrooms in this chapter.

Think art and accessories too. For example, a $5 garage-sale lamp can be personalized with a coat of paint and a few pictures of your teen's favorite musician or movie star. If it's a metal lamp, use magnetic clips to display photos or postcards that reflect your young adult's developing interests. Read on for more great ideas.

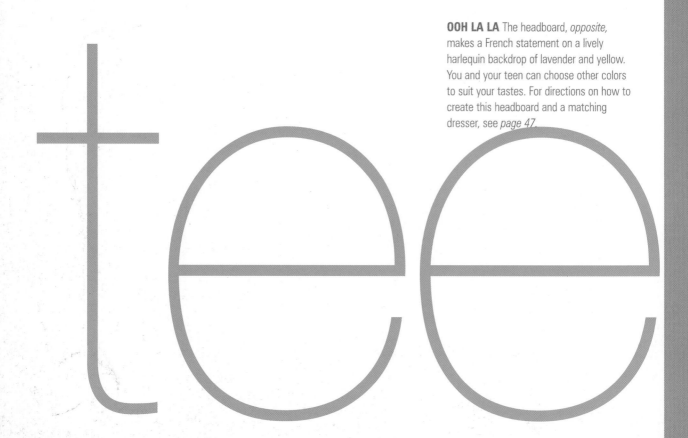

OOH LA LA The headboard, *opposite*, makes a French statement on a lively harlequin backdrop of lavender and yellow. You and your teen can choose other colors to suit your tastes. For directions on how to create this headboard and a matching dresser, see *page 47.*

promise them Paris

Have you ever been to Paris, the city of breezy boulevards, charming cafes, and the romantic Seine River? If your teen has a lust for travel or a love of things Parisian, this decorating theme may capture his or her imagination.

For this Parisian portrait bedroom, you'll need at least one basic mid-20th-century piece: A headboard or a dresser (free from family or around $30 each at garage sales). The bed and chest on these pages wear lavender and yellow. Choose your own colors to coordinate with the wall color.

THEY'LL ALWAYS HAVE PARIS An Eiffel Tower sketch adds the definitive French accent to the dresser and headboard, *below and opposite*. For a more traditionally masculine look, paint the dresser and headboard dark blue or black and paint the tower and harlequin shapes white.

create a Parisian headboard and dresser

Materials and Tools

Headboard and dresser	Paper
All-purpose cleaner	Flat sponges
Fine-grit sandpaper	Pencil
Tack cloth	Scissors
Stain-blocking primer/sealer	Paintbrushes
Flat acrylic latex paint: white,	Artist's round brush
yellow, pink, lavender, blue, and black	Matte-finish polyurethane

1 Clean the pieces with a diluted all-purpose cleaner.
2 Sand them with fine-grit sandpaper and wipe them clean with a tack cloth. Apply a layer of stain-blocking primer/sealer. Let dry. Apply a base coat of flat, white latex paint to pieces.
3 Choose a diamond size that suits the scale of the dresser. Cut a template out of paper and trace around it on a sponge. Cut out the shape from the sponge. Make several identical sponges, one for each paint color.
4 Practice sponging the shape on scrap paper. Then draw a line down the center of the dresser and headboard with a lead pencil.
5 At the top of the dresser and headboard, centering the sponge over the pencil line, sponge yellow diamonds all the way down the line. Apply remaining colors in the sequence shown, using a clean sponge for each color.
6 Referring to the photos on these pages, paint the trim, the dresser top and sides, and the footboard (if you have one).
7 Cut out a flower shape from a sponge and dip in pink paint. Sponge the top of the arch on each piece; let dry.
8 Lightly sketch the Eiffel Tower, squiggles, and French words in pencil. Using an artist's round brush, paint over your sketched lines with black paint.
9 Spray surfaces with matte-finish polyurethane; let dry.

For wall art, *left*, family photos are displayed in frames that have been painted to coordinate with the color scheme. (Similar frames are available at dollar stores.)

Here the frames are glued to long ribbons that hang from the wall on each side of the large window. You could use pictures of flowers instead of family photos to play up the garden theme.

Here are some other ways to bring a natural, breezy, garden feel to a teen's room for only a few dollars:

- **Hang worn windowpanes** on the wall to display photos. (Sometimes these are free for the taking at curbside on spring or fall cleanup days.)
- **Use dried grapevines** (about $6 at hobby stores or free after harvest at most vineyards) to soften the top of a window or the top of an armoire.
- **Tie a wide ribbon** that coordinates with the room colors to hold back curtains. Then attach dried baby's breath (about $3 a bunch at crafts stores) to the front of the ribbon with a hot-glue gun.
- **Buy a wooden bowl** at a discount store for around $10 and fill it with small gourds ($1 each) or leaves from your yard.
- **Fill an urn or vase** (less than $10 at discount stores) with bare branches from your backyard.
- **Purchase a large basket** made from twigs ($35 at home decorating stores) and use it to hold cozy pillows and blankets.

FLORAL FINDS Brightly colored flowers, *above left and opposite*, perk up any room. Cut them from your garden and let the bouquet be casual to keep the room relaxed.

go garden-fresh for less

Combine vintage pottery, botanical prints, and pretty colors to bring the relaxed charm of the garden into your teen's bedroom— for less cost than you'd imagine.

Decorating with a garden theme is a good way to save money. Low-cost floral fabrics, weathered-looking secondhand furniture, and homegrown or artificial flowers can turn any bedroom into a cozy haven for a teen who loves gardening or nature.

A wooden headboard, *above,* keeps the mood slightly rustic. The floral window treatment adds a touch of the garden. Painting the furniture white gives the whole room a fresh, breezy feeling.

how to
create a gardener's corner

Materials:

Pegboard	Seed packets
Decorative drawer pulls	Plants
Shower curtain	Gardening accessories

1 Hang a pegboard around one corner of the room.
2 Replace the pegs with decorative drawer pulls from your local hardware store.
3 Hang a shower curtain from the pulls.
4 Put seed packets along the top of the pegboard as decoration.
5 Set out plants, watering cans, gloves, or other gardening items to accessorize.

GROOVY GARDENER Highlight a teen's interest such as gardening, *below,* by adding thrifty touches—seed packets (3 for $1), a watering can (about $8), and floral drawer pulls ($3).

bring the outdoors in

Whether your teen is inspired by fishing, hiking, or relaxing on a beach, bedroom walls offer ample space to paint the perfect mood. A hand-painted mural like the one, *opposite,* will help make every day seem like a vacation.

If you're hesitant to paint the mural yourself, call your local community college. Ask an art instructor whether any art students are available to do the work for a minimal fee.

Props such as fishing poles, fishnets, life preservers, and colorful fishing lures are perfect inexpensive accessories for a fisherperson's room. Here are a few other ideas for adding outdoor touches:

- **Hang netting** (at retail outlet stores for about $25) as a window treatment. Glue tiny shells on the net for beautiful beach ambience.
- **Use an oar** (about $15-$25 in thrift shops) as a curtain rod. Drape it with beach towels, netting, or tab curtains, each available for under $25.
- **Stencil a nautical quote**, poem, or song around the top of the room for the minimal price of paints and brushes.
- **Use driftwood** from a nearby river for a towel bar or curtain rod (spray it for insects before you bring it inside).
- **Get bright picnic baskets** or large canvas bags, each around $20 at large retail stores, to stow teens' toiletries and cosmetic supplies.

BY THE SEA A vacation photo becomes a wall mural, *opposite.* Use a rented overhead projector to project a picture on the wall. Sketch a pencil outline and finish the scene with paints (around $10 per color).

GO RUSTIC Leather ties hold a curtain to a bamboo rod, *below.* Textured materials like these give a room tactile and woodsy appeal.

hot tip

A beach umbrella, around $25, and a lawn chair, about $15, can be turned into a special reading center in a teen's room that has a beach theme. Use plaster of Paris (sold in crafts stores for about $4 per bag) to fill a brightly colored container halfway; then insert the umbrella in the center of the mixture. Allow the plaster to dry. Fill up the rest of the pot with sand or small shells for an authentic beach feel.

howto
paint a mural

Materials and Tools

Overhead projector (check your local
schools or libraries to see whether
they check them out for free)
Vacation photo
Pencil for sketching
Paintbrushes
Paints

1 Use a copy machine to copy the
photo onto a transparency.
2 Place the transparency on the
overhead projector and sketch the
outline of the picture on the wall.
3 Fill in the outline with paint in the
desired colors.
4 Let dry.

PUMPED-UP PILLOWS The foam-core board, fiberfill, black pillowcases, and black paint needed for the project, *above,* cost about $25 at large discount stores. Get the feathers (under $1 each) at hobby stores.

display pillow-fight fun

In Colonial America, "shademakers" were peddlers who traveled the back roads creating pictures called silhouettes or shadowgraphs—an inexpensive alternative to oil portraits. Bring this style to life on your teen's bedroom wall for an exciting look that's amazingly affordable.

Here images of girls at a slumber party were outlined freehand on transparencies and then projected onto the wall with an overhead projector. Project your own images onto the wall, trace around them with a pencil, and fill in the outlines with black latex paint.

If drawing freehand makes you nervous, cut out subjects from actual photographs and tape them to transparencies. Project these onto the wall, again filling in with black latex paint, and you'll get the same dynamic effect.

This movement-filled mural includes swirling feathers and rumpled pillowcases that create a three-dimensional show. A hot-glue gun makes it easy to attach the pillows and feathers to the wall. Simple furnishings and

black and red accents set off the black silhouettes in this fantastic wall treatment.

Acrylic and latex paints dry fast, so squeeze only a little paint out of the tube at a time. If you're using a plastic palette, purchase a spray bottle and regularly spray a fine mist of water over the paint to rehydrate it. "Stay-wet" palettes are available in most art stores. On a "stay-wet" palette, the paint sits on a sheet of waxed paper placed on top of a damp piece of watercolor paper. This setup eliminates the need for rewetting the paint.

create a pillow-fight effect

Materials and Tools

Freehand sketches or cut out pictures of a pillow fight
Transparencies
Overhead projector
Pencil
1 quart of black latex or acrylic paint
Paintbrushes: 2-inch-wide brush and small artist's brush

Foam-core board
Utility knife
Hot-glue gun and glue sticks
Polyester fiberfill
2 to 4 pillowcases
Black and red feathers

1 Draw freehand sketches or cut out pictures of kids having a pillow fight and project them on the wall with an overhead projector, using transparencies.
2 Trace around the images with a pencil.
3 Fill in the outlines with a 2-inch-wide paintbrush, using black latex or acrylic paint.
4 Cut the pillow shapes from foam-core board with a utility knife.
5 Hot-glue fiberfill to the foam-core pillow shapes. Then hot-glue the pillowcases over the forms, wrapping and securing the fabric on the back of the foam-core.
6 Hot-glue the pillows and feathers to the wall. Then paint curved lines around the feathers with a small artist's brush to suggest motion.

have fun with fabulous fabrics

Fabric is a great way to add instant impact in a room without spending a fortune. Use it to introduce your teen's current favorite colors in pillows, artwork, or window treatments.

As your teen's tastes develop, swap out inexpensive fabric accessories instead of redoing the entire bedroom. It's OK to use more than one fabric pattern. For a unified look choose fabrics that have at least one color in common with the primary fabric.

When you change the colors of fabric accessories, consider the size and shape of the room. Think about how the placement of color will affect the overall sense of balance.

Finding a common hue in fabric color makes an enormous difference in how a room looks and feels. Too many colors or patterns can exhaust the eye and derail the room design.

Commonly, warm colors (yellow undertones) are used in large rooms to help make the space feel more cozy. Cool colors (blue undertones) or shades of white are often used in smaller rooms to help make the space seem bigger.

hot tip

To refresh your teen's bedroom each season without breaking your budget, choose neutral base colors for your scheme. Then add pastel pillows in the spring for a romantic mood. When summer comes, change accents such as vases or valances to vibrant reds, yellows, and navies. For autumn, use green, tan, and rust in floral arrangements. As winter sets in, introduce cozy colors, such as burgundy and spiced walnut, for throw rugs and other thrifty accents.

FAR EAST FOR LESS If your teen admires the exotic, the window treatment, *opposite,* may appeal. The sheer orange fabric (about $10 per yard) turns cold city sunlight into flaming desert sunset colors.

SAY IT WITH FLOWERS Fun retro-style fabric makes interesting wall art, *above.* Look for similar material on bargain tables at the fabric store. You'll need 2 yards of 54-inch-wide fabric. Make your own frame with 1×3 lumber and L-brackets. Wrap the fabric to the frame back and staple.

hot tip

If you have a large expanse of wall to decorate, look for complementary pictures or photos and display them as a group in similar frames. Together they'll work as well as one large piece of art. For a hip, contemporary look hang the pieces to form a square or rectangle.

VINTAGE FURNISHINGS The vintage white mesh chair, *above,* was a curbside treasure—picked up free on trash day. The table is simply a wooden packing crate from a grocery store (also free) turned upside down and painted white. The uneven boards and slightly rough texture add interest.

take advantage of vintage

Vintage is in and everything old is new again. From '40s costume jewelry to '50s dolls and '60s psychedelic fabrics, vintage looks are popular with many teens.

If your teen likes this look, get together and brainstorm what vintage items might work in his or her bedroom, from funky chairs to groovy accessories, such as retro chairs, tables, throw rugs, and pillows.

Consider jazzing up the walls with '50s to '70s movie posters, game boards, signs, or record albums. Many of these are colorful, fairly accessible, and under $25 at thrift shops or online at ebay.com.

It may be a shock to realize that items from your own teen years are now considered vintage. The consolation is that your teen may think you're supercool if you can unearth a few of these items and lend them to the room design.

If you don't have anything vintage, the next stop would be a fun day at a flea market, antique shops, or an estate sale. Keep an open mind—you may find a thrifty treasure that wasn't on your list that could "make" the entire room.

GROOVY BIKE A '50s bike, *right,* against the wall makes an almost architectural design statement. Good news: These are still available for under $25 at garage sales, junk shops, and flea markets. You probably can find a shelf similar to the retro one above the bike for less than $15 at a garage sale.

how to

make a "record guy or gal" poster

Materials and Tools

Large, unframed poster with a generic-looking man or woman
Hot-glue gun and glue sticks
Old record album
Frame for poster

1 Purchase a large, unframed poster that features a generic-looking man or woman in the print.
2 Hot-glue a record album over the face of the character.
3 Place the poster in a frame and hang on the wall.

RETRO ROCKS Use personal interests to turn a room into a haven. A simply shaped metal bed or headboard (about $45 from a thrift store) can "go retro" with spray paint, like the headboards and footboards, *above and opposite*. Retro prints for the wall are easy to find at thrift shops.

ACCENT ON ACCESSORIES A guitar, *opposite*, is a functional accessory that reveals a passion for music. A repainted garage-sale lamp ($5), *opposite*, sports a new shade ($8 at home discount stores) to create a funky, fun, frugal lamp for under $20.

go retro

An easy—and inexpensive—way to decorate teens' rooms is to use retro furnishings and accessories as shown on these pages. This style tends to be timeless, and the effect is fun and lively.

A blue palette was the starting point for this shared "retro rock 'n' roll" haven, *opposite and below*. Yard sales and flea markets are great places to find '60s and '70s retro pieces, such as the bedside lamp, *below*.

Translate some of the ideas in the bedrooms pictured here into great decor for your kids. You could use a credenza as a dresser, re-cover a bench cushion in colorful fabric, or revive a funky-shaped garage-sale lamp with metallic paint, *opposite*.

Display record album or CD covers as wall art ($1–$2 per cover at thrift shops). Or hang a brightly painted cup rack from the dollar store on the wall and use it to display retro jewelry that you and your teens discover together at thrift stores and garage sales.

how to
create a retro bed

Materials

Metal headboard in a retro style, similar to the ones below
Metal cleaner
Sandpaper for metal
Paint primer for meal
Spray paint for metal
Tools and fasteners for attaching the headboard to the frame

1 Purchase a metal headboard at a local flea market or used-furniture store (a footboard will cost extra; to keep expenses down, go without).
2 Clean and sand the headboard if needed. Prime the surface with a product made especially for metal.
3 Spray-paint the headboard with paint designed for use on metal. Let dry.
4 Attach the headboard to the bed frame. Touch up the paint if necessary.

reflect their individual interests. Have each choose a "signature color" within the chosen palette to help identify personal belongings and lounging areas.

- **Carve out personal space** for each person. All kids need a space of their own, whether it's for collectibles, homework, hobbies, or other projects. No matter how tight the space, make room for your teens' personal growth.
- **Install a curtain rod** on opposite sides of the room and hang a colorful shower curtain ($10–$25) as a simple, low-cost room divider.
- **For more privacy** move the beds to opposite sides of the room. Consider using different styles of beds and headboards to further differentiate the space.
- **A two-sided storage unit,** modular bookcases, or a large chalkboard on casters can help divide space.
- **Use multipurpose furniture** to minimize the clutter that crops up when two people share a room. Add underbed storage, stackable bins on rollers (about $10 at home discount stores) in the closet, and an armoire to house a computer.

hot tip

To make a teen's small room seem spacious, create a room divider of 12×48-inch door mirrors ($4 each), attaching them to each other with industrial strength glue. (You'll need six to eight mirrors for an average-size divider.) Prop them up with glass blocks.

divide and conquer

Even if your home is short on bedroom space, your teens still can stock up on style. Sharing a room can be a great learning experience for all involved and can help teach your teens how to negotiate.

If your kids are the same sex and near the same age, sharing a room can work well. To design a shared bedroom that runs smoothly, consider sleep schedules, privacy, and any other special needs. Here are a few other guidelines to help:

- **Working with your teens,** choose a color palette for the room. Then let each person choose designs, patterns, and linens to

CATCH A WAVE A folding screen like the one, *opposite,* can create a sense of privacy and help calm sibling storms with its idyllic seaside scene. Get your teens in on the act by asking them to choose and paint a scene that appeals to each of them.

THE GREAT DIVIDE Sheet metal, lumber, and faux glass, *above left,* make an inexpensive divider; however, you may need a carpenter to build a piece like this. The coffee table, *above left,* is sheet metal ($8) wrapped around two plywood disks ($18) and topped with lava rocks (about $16 a bag at hobby stores)—for a total of just $42.

how to
make a screen

Materials and Tools

Three 32×80-inch hollow-core interior doors
White interior latex paint
Hinges
Pencil

Paintbrush: 2-inch-wide
Three shades of interior latex paint
   in desired colors
Paintbrush: 1-inch-wide

1 Give the doors a base coat of white paint.
2 Hinge the doors together.
3 Using a pencil, draw waves on the screen, using this photo as a guide.
4 Using a 2-inch-wide brush, paint simple wave shapes with one of your three color choices. Fill in with the remaining colors, adding white to lighten and create subtle color changes with each brushstroke; let dry.
5 Highlight some of the wave shapes with the white paint, using a 1-inch-wide brush.

display their honors

Instead of sticking your teen's awards and honors in a drawer somewhere, consider displaying them as part of a wall-art piece in his or her bedroom.

An antique, weathered window such as the one, *above,* shows off ribbons for debate, 4-H, sports, speech, and drama. Windows of a slightly smaller scale often show up at farm or estate auctions or flea markets, so keep your eyes open for them.

Drive around neighborhoods on trash pickup days (you may need to check with your local waste management company to find out what

day these are). Sometimes items at the curbside are free for the taking—on a first-come, first-serve basis.

If you use a window, you may have room to set collectibles and awards inside the panes, as shown here. Positioning plaques, plates, and various other awards around the outside of the window anchors the piece, giving it a defined space on the wall.

HIGHLIGHT THEIR AWARDS Use an unusual weathered architectural piece, such as the antique window, *above,* to display your teens' honors and awards. If you can't find one you like for under $50 at a farm auction, check import shops and home-furnishing discount centers.

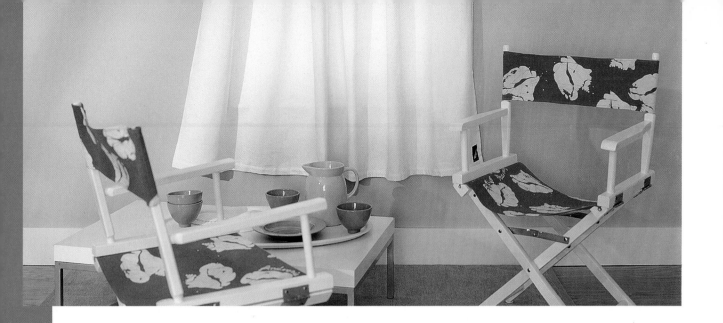

create $ensible chic with canvas

Canvas is trendy and economical—a convenient combo for a teen. Canvas represents the casual lifestyle teens love: It's down-to-earth yet ready for a spontaneous makeover. When kids tire of one look, the canvas quickly can take on a new color and design.

To take ordinary director's chairs from functional to fun, buy some acrylic paints for fabrics and some gesso (a compound that seals the surface and prepares it to accept paint) and turn that blank canvas into something bright and beautiful.

Consider the possibilities of other canvas surfaces. For example, you could buy four square canvas tote bags ($6–$7 each at discount stores) in different colors and paint or stamp a duplicate image on each one. Then hang them together on the wall as affordable modern art.

LIGHTS, CAMERA, ACTION Take two plain director's chairs, *above,* available at most retail stores for $8–$15 each, paint on designs, and turn a corner of your teen's room into a special reading, conversation, or project area.

paint a canvas director's chair

Materials and Tools

Canvas chair
Gesso
Paintbrushes

Latex or acrylic paint in desired colors
Cookie cutters
Sponges

1 Prime canvas with two coats of gesso; let dry. Clean the brushes thoroughly after using the gesso.
2 Apply two coats of acrylic paint as the base color; let dry.
3 Dip cookie cutters into the coordinating acrylic paint and press them on the canvas. Repeat the process with a damp sponge to create squares, rectangles, stars, or flowers.
4 Finish the design by filling in the stamped areas with paint and let the canvas dry overnight.

salvage great style

Shopping in salvage yards is a lot like shopping at garage sales or auctions: Once you find that absolutely perfect purchase, it makes the whole trip worthwhile.

With inexpensive items from a salvage yard, your teen's room can have the Eurostyle look that's so hot. Iron gates, columns, wall sconces, cornices, cherubs, and urns can add character to the room and change its entire mood. Some of the most appealing of these pieces are made of vintage wood. The more weathered the better, according to most hip designers.

You may find some wooden architectural items at flea markets for $10–$45 or for free at curbside on cleanup days. Leave these pieces untreated for a casual look or add new metal hinges and doorknobs for a more formal feel.

Turn an old discarded window into a fabulous piece of wall art by adding photos to the backside of the windows. Floral prints, family photos, or pictures from recent travels are all good options for turning a worn windowpane into a trip down memory lane. You can do this by gluing these mementos directly onto the glass panes.

Architectural elements such as the ones shown on these pages can add instant drama to any room. Contrasting textures, interesting designs, and jazzy junk capture the eye and the imagination. Peeling paint, chips, and rust hint at a past life, giving these pieces some extra fascination.

ADD AN ELEMENT Inject instant character with weathered architectural elements, *opposite*. If ones at salvage yards are too pricey, check import and home discount stores, where you can find faux ones for $3–$48.

SENSATIONAL SCONCES An aged antique wall sconce, *below*, available from salvage yards or flea markets for around $25, gives a sophisticated home to an ordinary plant.

For great pieces like the ones, *opposite,* check the Yellow Pages for a salvage yard. If none is listed, contact local remodeling or demolition firms and ask whether they sell elements scrapped from old buildings. If these are too costly, create your own. Display sections of old mesh or picket fences or apply special paint treatments to give new cornices, planters, and urns a vintage look.

use-what-you-have decor—for free

Low-cost decorating ideas are everywhere, and sometimes no-cost options are right under your nose. Using your teens' belongings and accessories to decorate their rooms costs nothing and captures your kids' style.

Consider the possibilities:

- **Hang empty frames** with no back and display your teen's favorite jewelry inside.
- **Use your teen's colorful beach towel** as a bedcover.
- **Hang out-of-service planting pots** near your teen's vanity to store skin care and hair products and grooming items.
- **If your teen loves gardening,** turn a wide windowsill into a display space. Fill small glass bottles with flowers and herbs and arrange them on the sill.
- **Fill a bowl with seashells** your teen gathered on vacation.
- **Use an expandable cup rack** ($1 at most dollar stores) to display your teen's colorful scarves or jewelry.
- **Repurpose your teen's favorite CD covers** into a fun decorating accent. Use metal clips to attach them to a nylon cord that matches the decor and drape the cord over the window valances.
- **Turn a peg rack** into wall art by hanging clean towels, hats, or shirts.
- **Transform ordinary metal objects** such as desks, lamps, and frames into display areas. Use magnetic clips from office supply stores to hang photos, greeting cards, or invitations.

CLIP 'N' GO Magnetic clips, *right,* can turn any metal surface into a delightful display. They cost about $5 for a set of four at most office-supply stores.

BEACH BLANKET BEAUTY A beach hat and colorful towels, *opposite far left,* make like wall art when hung together.

WEARABLE ART A teen's colorful camisoles, tops, and shirts, *opposite,* can act as art if they're displayed with flair.

If you've always wanted to create your own window coverings, now is the time to start. Creating window treatments for kids' rooms is fun and easy, whether you're into bold primary colors or the soft whites and taupes of a beach scene.

Be creative. Buy inexpensive items from flea markets, garage sales, or thrift stores and incorporate them in your window treatments. Line windowsills with pre-owned toys or stuffed animals. Use colorful scarves as valances or enhance curtains with fanciful trims on sale at your local fabric store. Let a limited budget unleash your imagination and you'll create one-of-a-kind style for your one-of-a-kind kid.

WINDOW DISPLAY Window treatments that incorporate displays, *opposite and left*, add interest to a room and solve storage dilemmas, especially for collectibles such as seashells or jewelry. In the treatment *opposite,* ordinary wire wraps around the bottle necks and attaches to curtain rings with clips.

use nature's beauty for a bargain

hot tip

If you can't find a bit of Mother Nature in your own neighborhood, contact a local tree service. It may offer a variety of branches and other foliage at a fraction of the cost of artificial items. Spray any such material for insects before you bring it inside. Also check with local parks departments. If they have damaged trees, they may give you permission to take the broken branches home. Check out save-on-crafts.com or ebay.com— websites that offer inexpensive artificial foliage.

As you look through this chapter for ideas, consider this: Extraordinary window treatments may be right in your own backyard. Bring a little of the outdoors in by using free natural materials in your window decorating schemes.

Designers are turning to these items in an effort to recycle and as a way of honoring natural resources. If your goal is to create a serene, soothing room for your baby, grade-schooler, or teen, use fallen branches, logs, or vines to top a window, a technique shown *on these pages.*

Work with natural colors, shades of white, and wood tones. Then introduce layered textures to help re-create the variety found in the outdoors.

HEARD IT THROUGH THE GRAPEVINE
Woven grapevines ($10 at local crafts stores) top this window treatment *below and opposite.* Check flea markets for a bedspread similar to the white-on-white chenille one used here. For $20–$30, it could be a bargain drapery in disguise.

romance it with ribbons

The treatment in this room creates a perfect bedroom haven for a girl, preteen or teen who likes a traditionally feminine look. The blue wallcovering gives the entire room a soothing backdrop of color. White woodwork and trim throughout the room gives the eye a rest from the blue patterns and adds a sense of freshness.

The window treatment is the showstopper. A wide tailored valance shows off the large-scale sage and periwinkle plaid fabric. A laced bow in a coordinating fabric that matches the drapes ties the look together at the center of the valance.

MIX 'N' MATCH Blue and green tones in four different patterns, *opposite,* work together to give this room charm and excitement. Look for inexpensive coordinating fabrics (about $5 a yard) to make items such as the valance, matching pillows, and table cover.

WRAP IT UP The valance, *left,* wraps up the window treatment with a laced bow down the center. Wide satin ribbon costs about $3 per yard; if you prefer, make your own laced bow out of inexpensive fabric.

make a ribboned window treatment

Materials and Tools

Measuring tape	Ruler
Handsaw	Chalk
1×4-inch wood board	Contrasting fabric ribbon
Sewing scissors	Staples and staple gun
45-inch-wide fabric	L-brackets
Iron and ironing board	Screws
Sewing machine capable of making buttonholes	Screwdriver
Matching threads	

1 Measure the width of the window and add 2 inches. Cut the 1×4-inch wood board to this measured length.
2 Cut a length of 45-inch-wide fabric to equal the width of the window frame plus 20 inches.
3 In the center, fold the fabric in half lengthwise, with right sides facing. Iron in a sharp crease.
4 Stitch together the edges with a ½-inch seam allowance, leaving an opening for turning. Clip the corners, turn right sides out, and press. Slip-stitch the opening closed.
5 Fold a box pleat and slip-stitch the folds in place. Using a ruler and chalk, mark ½-inch vertical slits at 2-inch intervals along each side of the box pleat.
6 Stitch buttonholes over the marks and slit the buttonholes open.
7 Lace the contrasting fabric ribbon through the buttonholes.
8 Using a staple gun, staple the top of the box pleat to the top center of the precut 1×4-inch board. Then staple the rest of the valance to the top of the board, working out to each end.
9 Wrap the fabric around the ends of the board. Staple in place. Trim off excess fabric wrap. Mount L-brackets above the window frame. Attach the covered cornice board to the L-brackets with screws.

hot tip

Before you start brainstorming which looks you want for your windows, consider privacy and sun control. Do you need window treatments that can be opened and closed? Will they need lining? Also consider how the room relates to others in your home. Basic styles such as drapery panels or shades work in many settings, depending on the fabrics, trims, and detailing you choose.

tie up great savings

Window treatment tiebacks serve a dual purpose: They're functional and decorative. By drawing draperies and curtains to one side, they allow light to permeate a room. Conventional and nonconventional resources and a variety of styles are available to help spark your imagination. And because tiebacks can be fashioned from almost any object, the decorating possibilities are many.

Let your kids' interests, collections, or hobbies inspire your choice of tiebacks. Small wooden trains threaded together on a cord make a perfect train-track loop around a curtain. Colorful pink or red bandannas, ($1–$3 each at drugstores), draped over a curtain rod can give a Western-themed room an authentic look (and no sewing required). Though inexpensive, tiebacks can change the look of a room in a mere instant. Here are some out-of-the-ordinary tie-backs that can be found almost anywhere:

- **Buy a length of chain** at your local hardware store for a funky way to tie back curtains or draperies in teens' rooms. If you like, paint it to match one of the room colors.
- **Buy lace or ribbon** on sale at a fabric store to create charming tiebacks in a girl's or preteen's room.
- **Use decorative napkin rings** in the shapes of animals to help corral curtains in kids' rooms.
- **Tie curtains with colorful scarves,** plain or printed, in a teen's room. For guy teens, use retro men's ties from The Salvation Army or DAV—they're only a buck or two each, and they don't even have to match.
- **Attach toy ornaments** with a hot-glue gun to plain white tiebacks for a colorful holiday treatment.

hot tip

When using any type of cording or rope as a tieback, secure it high enough so that it's out of the reach of children and pets.

how to

make nautical tiebacks

Materials

Large screws   Cleats   White nylon cord

1 With large screws (or toggle bolts if you can't screw into studs) fasten the cleats, *above,* to the wall 6 inches above the window frame and 4 inches from each side.
2 Thread the cord through the grommets in the curtain panel and wrap the ends of the cord around the cleats, nautical style.
3 If the cord droops, release and rewrap it to get the look you want.
4 Trim the ends of the cord and tie each end in a simple knot.

NAUTICAL TREASURES Check local boat-supply stores for nautical hooks, *above,* ($3–$10). If the selection is too small, place a special order. While you're there, buy nautical cord ($10–$15) to secure curtains.

CHENILLE CHIC This stylish tieback, *opposite and left,* is cut from a secondhand chenille bedspread and trimmed with yellow fabric ($2–$4 a yard at fabric stores) for a cheery look. Look for bargains on chenille bedspreads at garage sales and thrift stores.

bag valance values

When you're decorating a window on a budget, valances are ideal. Draperies can cost hundreds of dollars for a small window, while valances are about $12–$20 at most home discount stores. Use them alone when privacy isn't a factor or combine them with shades or blinds when it is. Then you'll have the option of pulling the cord to hide the blind or adjusting the shade to direct sunlight into the room.

Originally designed to hide window hardware, valances can be used to tie together windows and doors of different shapes and sizes. A loosely hung valance conveys a casual mood; a tailored one is more formal. A little extravagance in the amount of material—doubling or tripling the width of the window—creates a luxurious look when you gather the fabric.

For low-cost impact consider adding fringe, covered buttons, or matching-fabric trims to the bottom or sides of a valance. Drape colorful strands of beads over a valance to add a bit of excitement to any diva's window.

Or stitch crystal trim to the bottom edges of a valance for extra shine and sparkle. For a more traditionally masculine look, attach wooden beads, strips of leather, or toy trains to the valance.

IN THE BAG Top the window of a teen shopper with a valance of colorful bags, *opposite*, available from dollar stores. Other inexpensive options: kids' cowboy hats ($3 each) hung along a curtain rod or a feathery boa ($7–$8) draped at the top of a window.

GLASS BEADS Beaded trim, *below*, dresses up an inexpensive valance, giving it an elegant look. The trim costs $3–$6 a yard at sewing centers. Use fusible tape to adhere the trim if you don't sew.

If you use reversible fabrics on either side of the valance, you'll be able to change the look at a moment's notice. Use small prints that have a pattern you can see from a short distance away. Then from farther away, the pattern will appear simply as a splash of color. Choose the same fabric in two different shades or colors to add a slight twist to a simple style.

sew with bed linens and save

Bargain sheets can be found at flea markets, garage sales, antique fairs, discount stores, and online auctions. Check these websites for bed linen bargains:

smartbargains.com

domesticbin.com

designerlinensoutlet.com

homegoods.com

overstock.com

domestications.com

linensource.com

thecompanystore.com

shopping-bargains.com

Bed linens are affordable and come in a wonderful array of colors and patterns to match any decor. They're easy to care for and can coordinate with dust ruffles, duvets, and pillows.

In the room, *opposite,* swing rods and fun fabrics create a hip, retro look. To make this window treatment, take two pillowcases (this pair cost $7 at an antique shop), slip a layer of drapery lining ($3 per yard) inside to help block the pattern show-through, and then sew a rod pocket near the closed end.

Leave an inch of fabric for a ruffle above the rod. At the open end of the case, attach scalloped felt trim along the hemline. Then with a hot-glue gun, attach white cording on top of the trim.

Before embarking on this project, measure your window carefully. Also look for cases with decorative hems; then you'll have to add only the rod pocket. When looking for discount linens, remember that the quality depends on the fiber of the fabric. A higher thread count usually means softer and more durable material.

Always hand-wash vintage linens with mild soap; rinse thoroughly. Then line-dry them before ironing them on low heat.

REAL RETRO Swing-arm curtain rods (about $20 at home improvement stores), *opposite,* help give this room a fun look.

PILLOWCASE POTENTIAL Find pillowcases such as the one, *above,* for $4-$15 a pair at home discount stores or for $1–$3 at garage sales or thrift stores.

A WHITER SHADE OF PALE The plain white shades, *above,* help break up the intensity of the blue and red patterns in this bedroom. They're thrifty, too, at just $10–$15 each at most home discount centers.

think: white is all right

Sometimes a softly serene room, *right,* can benefit from a white or off-white window treatment to keep the mood mellow. White window treatments also can provide a fresh, crisp feeling when paired with bright or medium shades of blue and red, *opposite.*

You can put together an economical and effortless window covering using pleated paper shades, *right.* They're a tasteful, temporary alternative to more costly window treatments, and they diffuse light beautifully.

Paper shades come ready to hang by self-adhesive edges. Usually they're hung horizontally; however, if you turn the panels sideways, they become permanent curtains with vertical pleats.

PLEATED PAPER Paper shades, *right,* are known as temporary shades in home center language. They work well for homes with small children or pets and cost only $10–$15.

how to
install a paper shade

Materials and Tools

Measuring tape	36-inch-long threaded rod
Paper shades	Finial nuts
Scissors	2-inch-wide screw eyes
Paper punch	

1 To trim the shade, measure from the sill to three-fourths of the window height.
2 Mark the length lightly across the pleats and cut, three at a time, with sharp scissors.
3 Use a paper punch to make holes along the edge, punching through three pleats at a time and using a previous hole as a guide.
4 To hang the panel, insert a 36-inch-long threaded rod through the holes; the threads separate the pleats.
5 Screw finial nuts on the rod ends and hang the rod on 2-inch-wide screw eyes.

how to
embellish paper shades

Materials and Tools

Art papers in desired colors and designs	Spray adhesive
Paper shades	Screw eyes
At least 3 colors of natural handmade papers	Hanging wire
Scissors	Binder clips
Decorative trims as desired	

1 Purchase natural handmade art papers from local art or specialty paper stores ($5-$12). These stores offer a wide variety of styles and colors to match any scheme.
2 Cut paper to fit the size of the window. Use one color as the background.
3 Cut shapes from coordinating handmade papers to create a visual picture on the window.
4 Lay out shapes on the paper shades before gluing them in place. Add decorative trims to enhance the look.
5 Attach cutouts by lightly spraying them with an adhesive spray. After adhering the cutouts let the adhesive dry.
6 To hang the shade put screw eyes into the wall on each side of the window opening; string wire between them. Then attach the paper to the wire with binder clips.

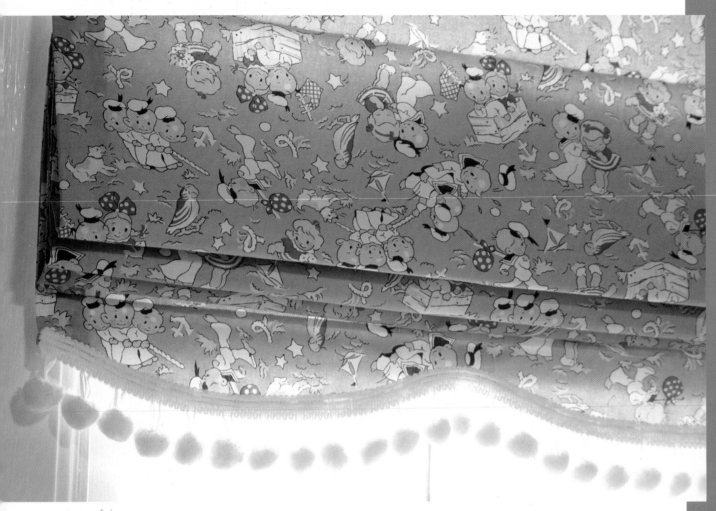

hot tip

Add decorative trims such as beaded or ball fringe to the bottom of the shade for an extra touch of personality. Purchase a denim shade for a bit of country character and add suede fringe for an outback mood.

go a shade better

An adaptable classic, the roller shade is a longtime favorite window covering. Local discount stores carry standard roller shades for $5–$10 and custom shades for about $30.

With the variety of trims now available in fabric stores—from lace to flowers to rickrack—you quickly can embellish window shades to fit the decor and colors of your kid's room. Purchase material that goes with the room colors, cut out strips or portions of it, and use a hot-glue gun to adhere it to the shade.

If you're an artist at heart, you may want to paint a design on the shade, with your child or teen helping you. Coordinate your color scheme before attempting the real thing. Look in local crafts or discount stores for stencils ($2–$10) if you're reluctant to paint freehand.

POM-POM POWER White pom-pom trim ($3–$5 a yard at fabric stores), *opposite*, dresses up a nursery shade. The trim was attached with a hot-glue gun.

ANIMALS ON PARADE The breezy pull-down shade, *above*, matches the animal fabric on the throw pillows and bed. You can get the same effect by using a hot-glue gun to adhere colorful animal fabric ($3–$6 a yard at fabric stores) to a plain white roll-down shade ($5–$10 at home discount centers).

use trims for thrifty makeovers

An economical pre-made or handmade window treatment can stay stylish with periodic makeovers. Adding trims or interesting hardware can update the look for very little money.

When choosing trim, play off the fabric to enhance the look. Beads, lace, tassels, ribbon, buttons, and even feathers—these are a few "trims of the trade" to get you started. Trims are generally inexpensive and provide a quick fix for any window covering you can imagine. Consider these ideas:

- **Adorn the triangular tips** of a berry-print pennant-style valance with clusters of artificial berries.
- **Sew colorful jumbo buttons** along the vertical hemline of a neutral drapery panel.
- **Use ribbon-tied bows** instead of the usual rings to secure a drapery.

Consider, too, how hardware can help transform a treatment from plain to perfect. Rods can be wood, iron, brass, or even clear acrylic, allowing you to create a number of styles.

Decide first whether you want your hardware to fade into the background or to make a design statement. Search for a style that will bring out the best in your window and create a custom look for a lot less than retail prices.

ROMANTIC GLOW A string of miniature lights ($5–$7) drapes over a curtain rod, *below and opposite,* creating a lovely effect. The plastic hoods ($8–$12) are available at shops that specialize in party lights.

hot tip

Update a wooden rod by painting it black or another color to match your decor. Choose fabric that coordinates with the hardware. Here are some websites that offer a variety of fabric trims and hardware at minimal cost:

mjtrim.com

wholesaletrims.com

denverfabrics.com

bizrate.com

target.com

add cheer with flowers

This '60s-style window treatment is bold, unique, and fun. Here a pink, green, and white plaid window covering starts out basic and takes on a whole new look with easy-to-do flower appliqués.

It all starts with a box-pleated valance in fabric matching the comforter, *opposite,* and that coordinates with the wall color and floor covering. Then the valance is jazzed up with colorful daisy appliqués, starting at around $1.50 each at most fabric stores. The window also can be customized with points of lace, a kind of "petticoat for the valance" peeking out from the lower edge. Hang a lacy sheer underneath to get this special effect.

PRETTY IN PLAID This blast-from-the-past window topper, *opposite and below,* works well because it helps coordinate the color scheme throughout the room. When the sun shines in, sheer panels help filter the light. They're available online at domestications.com for about $15.

hot tip

Use patterned sheer draperies for added interest. Or invent your own design on plain sheers, using stencils and fabric paints, applied sparingly. Layer sheers in varying colors that complement the room; they'll add privacy without reducing light. Tie back one panel to allow the other color to show through. Visit bizrate.com and domestications.com for more inexpensive window options.

create clever curtain rods

Don't let your imagination stop at window treatments. Think about clever—and inexpensive—curtain rods too. Here are ideas you might try:

- **Buy a length of PVC pipe** at your local hardware store to serve as a curtain rod. Add PVC elbows to each end. For a funky, hip mood, leave it uncovered. Or cover it with fabric for a more finished look.
- **For a romantic treatment,** find a twig or slight branch a little wider than your window and drape gauze or scarves over it for a low-cost but elegant feel. You also can paint the twig or branch in a color to coordinate with the room.
- **Lengths of bamboo,** available at most hobby and crafts stores, can make unusual curtain rods, especially when used with earth-toned, woven, or nubby curtains. They also can help create an exotic look when paired with animal or leopard prints.
- **Simple tension rods** make fun, low-cost curtain rods and come in a variety of sizes and colors.
- **Heavy rope in red or navy** can add a jaunty, nautical look when used as rods with red, white, and blue curtains.
- **For a girl who loves the "diva" look,** braid three or more strands of pastel beads together to hold lace sheers in place.

Smart, budget-conscious decorators everywhere are using paint to transform kids' rooms and furniture—and no wonder: Less than $50 buys enough paint to cover an average-size kid's room or several pieces of bedroom furniture. Whether you and your kids are into lavender and lace or bold checks and geometric designs, you'll find inspiration in this chapter.

rule with rickrack

If you need ideas for decorating, think of trims and embellishments that could inspire a theme or color palette. Here rickrack trim sets the theme for a painted dresser, a headboard, and the border at the top of the wall. Shades of lilac draw attention to the drawer fronts, finished with white ceramic pulls. The deeper lilac is duplicated in the stenciled rickrack, providing contrast for the dresser top and sides.

To get other ideas for bedroom design themes, you and your youngster or teen may want to pursue these activities:

- **Visit a florist's shop** to discover interesting shapes, textures, and colors.
- **Stroll through your local art center** and discuss which artwork attracts you and why.
- **Purchase current decorating books and magazines** and mark the pictures that appeal to you.

how to
paint a nightstand

Materials and Tools

Nightstand
Medium- and fine-grit sandpaper
Tack cloth
Paintbrushes
Interior latex paint: lemon yellow, light lilac, dark lilac, light pastel green, and white

Daisy stamps in two sizes
Rickrack stencil
Repositionable spray adhesive
Matte-finish, clear polyurethane

1 Sand the nightstand with medium-grit and then with fine-grit sandpaper. Wipe with a tack cloth.
2 Paint the top, sides, and bottom panel yellow; paint the legs light green.
3 Paint the drawer fronts. Create a checkerboard effect by painting the drawer fronts two shades of lilac.
4 Detail the top. Stamp daisies in white, using two sizes of commercial stamps. Let dry. Stamp again in lilac, slightly outside the first stamped lines.
5 Stencil the rickrack lilac. Affix a 4-inch section of the stencil to the furniture surface with repositionable spray adhesive. Adjust the stencil on the nightstand as needed to complete the design.
6 Allow the painted surfaces to dry for at least two days between each step. Seal with clear matte-finish polyurethane.

BRIGHT AND BEAUTIFUL This playfully painted nightstand, *opposite*, holds a bright floral lamp, a functional accent piece.

get the blues

Blues music and blue rooms have something in common: Depending on the style, both can range from calming to intense. Light blue has a soothing effect and makes a room seem light and open. Dark blue tends to be cozier and more dramatic.

If you want to match a solid-color blue fabric, ask whether your local paint dealer can custom-mix a shade. A color's value refers to how light or dark it is. Yellow is the lightest, and purple is the darkest.

To make a room look larger and more spacious you'd use a lighter value of the color. To make a room seem smaller and more intimate, you'd choose a darker value.

A STELLAR CHOICE Midnight blue walls, *below,* are a perfect backdrop for stenciled stars. The bright yellow bedspread adds a lighter note.

UNDER THE SEA Giant sea creatures join seaweed and coral, *opposite,* creating a seaworthy style that's easy to customize for boys and girls.

how to
paint starry walls

Materials and Tools

Star template in several different sizes
Clear acetate sheets
Fine-tip marker
Cutting mat
Utility knife

Latex paint: midnight blue
Paintbrush: 3-inch-flat
Acrylic stenciling cream: sparkling white
Stenciling brush
Sea sponge

1 Purchase or create a star template. To make the template, find a star shape and use a photocopy machine to enlarge or reduce it different sizes as desired.
2 Place clear acetate over each star. Use a fine-tip marker to trace the outline onto the acetate.
3 Working on a cutting mat, cut out the stencil designs with a utility knife.
4 Paint walls with two or more coats of midnight blue paint with a 3-inch-wide, flat paintbrush until you have a uniform look; let dry.
5 Using sparkling white acrylic stenciling cream and a stenciling brush, stencil stars of varying sizes onto the wall in a random fashion.
6 While the stenciled stars are still wet, use a damp sea sponge to soften the edges, creating a glowing, halo-like effect.

create a seascape

Materials and Tools

Painter's tape

Paintbrushes

Latex paints: light blue, medium blue, white, yellow, bright orange, green, white, purple, and any other colors you want to paint the tropical fish

Sea sponge

White chalk

Black, fine-tip permanent marker

Artist's paintbrushes

Flat polyurethane

1 Mask off the walls and paint the ceiling light blue. Sponge-paint white clouds onto the ceiling. If desired add birds and a smiling sun.

2 Mask off the ceiling and paint the walls medium blue. Uneven painting with dark and light spots will create a watery look.

3 Outline the fish and coral with white chalk. Fill in the outlines with bright colors and simple patterns. After the paint dries, outline the details on the sea life with a permanent marker.

4 Using white chalk, outline strands of seaweed and fill the outlines with green paint.

5 Using a natural sea sponge and white latex paint, add depth with underwater bubbles and foam.

6 Seal the walls with flat polyurethane.

go dynamic

Toss out the notion that pink is for girls and blue is for boys. Most kids love bright, bold, and multicolor schemes. Many parents start with a favorite color (theirs or the child's) and work from there, adding heavy doses of contrast. Fun patterns can emerge, often inspired by children's artwork or folk art.

When working with bold colors, always balance the bright with white. Too much color can be overpowering, especially in a small room. If you use patterns, stick with a theme: geometrics or florals, for example, to help hold the room together.

SHOWSTOPPER Color and pattern make this secondhand dresser, *opposite and right*, the star of the room. While the colors share the same intensity, doses of white offer visual relief. The patterns are geometric, done in folk art style for a casual look.

paint a bold dresser

Materials and Tools

Dresser
Sandpaper
Commercial stripper (if needed)
Tack cloth
Primer (stain-blocking, if needed)
Paintbrushes
Brown paper bag

Flat latex paint: white, red, blue, purple, green, and yellow
Paper
Erasable pencil
Ruler
Small, stiff-bristle artist's brushes
Water-base polyurethane

1 If the dresser was previously painted or most of the finish is gone, ordinary sanding will do. For varnished and enamel surfaces, use a commercial stripper to remove the slick finish, and follow the instructions and safety precautions exactly. Then sand. Wipe away sanding dust with a tack cloth.

2 Prime all surfaces; let dry. Then give them a light rubbing with a brown paper bag to remove any raised grain. If there are surface stains, use a stain-blocking primer. Paint the chest with a base coat of flat white latex.

3 Practice your patterns on paper to develop the style you like best. Select a variety of related patterns, such as the stars, stripes, diamonds, and dots shown here.

4 Note the natural design lines and breaks of the piece and determine which pattern will go on each section. Paint each section with the base color that will be the background. (On sections where the white shows through, white is the background color, and the other color is added on top.) Let the paint dry.

5 Using an erasable pencil and a light touch, draw the designs onto the dresser. For straight lines and evenly spaced segments such as the diamonds or stripes, use a ruler as a guide but paint freehand over the lines.

6 Fill in the outlined designs with the accent colors, using small, stiff-bristle artist's brushes. After the paint dries, seal the dresser with water-base polyurethane.

make it fun

Using a theme that matches your child's interests is a natural way to personalize his or her room. Dinosaurs are the theme du jour in the room shown here. Choose your theme and then look for a used headboard and toy chest at thrift shops or garage sales. A few flaws in the finish are OK; you'll be painting over them.

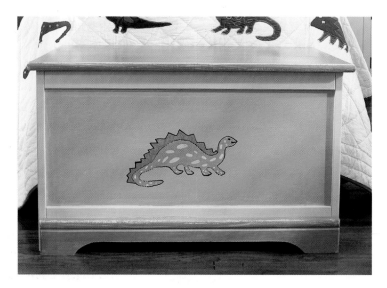

Look for bedding that fits your theme and use that as your starting point. If none exists, use solid-color bedding and look for patterned wallcovering instead.

Here a dinosaur comforter inspires the stenciled picture on the toy chest. The headboard takes on the look of prehistoric geologic layers.

Both surfaces have an aged finish that is created by sanding the top coat so the base color shows through. Rubbing a candle along edges that would be likely to receive wear helps keep the top coat from adhering and allows the base coat to show through.

DYN-O-MITE DECOR These projects, *left and opposite,* are easy to paint. The dinosaur on the toy chest is traced from the bedspread pattern. The layers on the headboard are freehand, painted over light pencil sketching.

how to
paint a toy chest

Materials and Tools

Toy chest
Sandpaper
Tack cloth
Acrylic latex paint: pale green, navy, red, orange, blue, lilac, and yellow
Paintbrushes
Dinosaur pattern

Clear stencil plastic
Black fine-tip permanent marker
Piece of glass larger than the dinosaur pattern
Utility knife
Repositionable spray adhesive
Matte-finish water-base polyurethane

1 Sand the chest, wipe it with a tack cloth, and paint it pale green; let dry.
2 Following the natural breaks and lines of the toy chest and using the photograph, *above,* as a guide, paint the inside navy, the lid red, the front orange, and the front bottom panel blue; let dry. Lightly sand the surfaces and wipe them with a tack cloth.
3 Find a dinosaur pattern and enlarge it to the desired size on a photocopy machine. Place clear stencil plastic over the pattern and trace two dinosaurs, using a black fine-tip permanent marker. Lay the stencil plastic on a piece of glass. Using a utility knife, cut out the dinosaur body for one stencil and the spines for the second stencil.
4 Spray the backside of the stencils with repositionable spray adhesive. Center the body stencil on the front of the toy chest and paint the body lilac. Allow the paint to dry; then center the spine stencil over the body and paint the spines red.
5 After the paint dries add yellow spots. Outline the body and the spines with a fine-tip permanent marker. Add the eye and the smile.
6 Allow the paint to dry and then seal with matte-finish water-base polyurethane.

Quality products save you time. If you're using good-quality paint and the best rollers and brushes you can afford, the paint will go on much more smoothly and evenly and will give you better coverage.

paint a headboard

Materials and Tools
Headboard
Medium- and fine-grit sandpaper
Tack cloth
Acrylic latex pale green, forest green, navy, red, orange, blue, lilac, and yellow

Paintbrush: 2-inch-wide tapered
Matte-finish water-base polyurethane

1 Sand the headboard with medium-grit sandpaper, wipe it with a tack cloth, and paint it pale green; let dry. Using a 2-inch-wide tapered paintbrush, add horizontal waves in contrasting colors. The waves do not have to be exact or opaque; some of the base coat can show through. Let the paint dry.
2 Add narrow forest green waves; detail them with vertical navy dashes; let dry.
3 Lightly sand the headboard with fine-grit sandpaper so the finish looks slightly aged. Sand more thoroughly along the edges and in spots that naturally would receive the most wear.
4 Wipe the surface clean with a tack cloth. Seal it with matte-finish water-base polyurethane.

paint a flower border

Materials and Tools

Yardstick   Stiff-bristle artist's brush
Pencil   Flat latex paint: pale green, pale blue, and pale pink

This project involves a reverse-painting method: The border is painted around the flower shapes and dots so the background wall color shows through on the petals and along the rim of each dot. Note how the uneven painting technique lets the base coat show through, tying the look together and adding to the fanciful feel of the room.

1 Using a yardstick and pencil, measure up from the floor to mark where you want the bottom of the border. Standard chair rail height is 32 to 34 inches from the floor; adjust this measurement to your room so the border works well with the height of the furniture and windows. Lightly draw a solid line to connect the marks and create the bottom of the border.

2 Draw the top border in the same manner, placing it about 8 inches above the bottom line. Measure and mark dots every 9 inches along the center of the border. These will be the flower and dot centers.

3 Using a pencil and a light touch, draw alternating flowers and dots at the marked spots. With a small stiff-bristle artist's brush, outline the flowers and dots with the border paint.

4 Paint the border up to the outlines. Use flat strokes for the top and bottom of the border; then fill in the center with random brushstrokes that allow a bit of the base coat to show through.

5 Paint the flower centers with a second color. For the dots use a third color and leave a rim of the background color around each one.

pick some flower power

Flowers are a perennial favorite with many girls of all ages, including teens, and retro-look daisies and dots are popping up like wildflowers in many rooms. Apple green, pink, blue, and citrus colors have replaced the orange, gold, and brown of the '70s for an update to an old favorite. It's breezy, bright, and fun.

STYLIZED SAVVY To keep a lighthearted feel, draw stylized flowers freehand, *below and opposite.* If you're intimidated by drawing, ask your kids to pitch in and help. Directions for creating this border appear *opposite, below.*

Paint won't adhere to damp surfaces, so check that your walls are dry before applying paint. If weather dampens the walls, run an air-conditioner or dehumidifier or wait for more favorable conditions to paint. For walls that routinely draw dampness, such as basement ones, use a water-blocking base coat.

go from blah to beautiful

Here, *right and opposite,* the stars of the room are pattern and color, not expensive furniture. Who knows? The happy atmosphere even may act as an antidote to some of those teen moods.

In this bedroom, *right,* wide, alternating strips of two shades of blue paint spark interest and make a lively contrast to the pinks and greens used in the fabrics. The bold hot pink and red color scheme with its jolts of color and hip attitude, *opposite,* is likely to be a hit with preteens and teens. It's a great example of daring to use wildly contrasting colors, if the effect fits the mood you're trying to create.

SOME LIKE IT HOT The mod look, *opposite,* is created with hot pink walls and red furniture and frames. The white and chrome tables help break up the intensity. You could easily substitute white plastic patio tables for $15–$25 or white beanbag chairs for around $19 from home discount stores.

MIX IT UP Dare to mix stripes, checks, and florals and other patterns for a cheery, upbeat mood, such as in this room, *right.*

paint striped walls

Materials and Tools

Premium-bond primer
Two shades of latex wall paint
Paintbrushes
Measuring tape
Pencil
Carpenter's level
Painter's masking tape for decorative painting

1 Decide how wide you want the stripes (2 to 4 inches works well in most rooms).
2 Prime walls with a premium-bond primer. After they dry, paint on a base coat. Allow to dry to avoid smudging.
3 Measure and mark stripes on the wall with a pencil, using the level to ensure straight lines. Don't erase or you'll smudge the wall.
4 Mask off every other stripe with tape, as follows. Carefully mask the outer edge of each pencil mark with quality painter's masking tape. Tightly seal down the edge next to the pencil lines with your fingers to prevent the paint from bleeding through. Test a small area first to be safe.
5 Paint the stripes of bare wall exposed in between the masked-off stripes. Use smooth, even strokes.
6 After the color is applied, gently remove the tape before the paint dries, being careful not to smear it.

Whatever paint techniques you use, practice them before putting any paint on the wall. If possible work on a piece of primed drywall or smooth plywood that is at least 3 to 4 feet square. Paint over each trial run until you've perfected the technique.

add new character

Furniture takes on an artistic appeal when it becomes the "canvas" for creative painting. Visit an art fair and you'll find that painted and patterned furniture is hot—and pricey. Get your own custom look for a fraction of the cost by revamping furniture that's been hiding in the basement or attic, hanging around a thrift store, or languishing at curbside.

Look for pieces that are structurally sound. Check the joints, drawers, and basic construction. Minor repairs are no problem; rickety pieces are better left behind. You're likely to find something nicer around the corner.

Also check for stains that may bleed through the paint and do a sniff test for musty or unpleasant odors.

If you have a piece with lots of visual interest and detailing such as finials, beveled edges, and ornate trim, consider a block-painting design, which features separate colors for the different segments of the piece. Heavily patterned designs work best on furniture that has straight lines and little detailing.

CHECK IT OUT Surface preparation is important when you're painting used furniture like the colorful chest, *above,* and child's chair, *opposite.* Sand previously painted pieces with medium- and fine-grit sandpaper and wipe with a tack cloth to remove dust. This ensures a smooth surface for new paint.

how to
paint a patterned dresser

Materials and Tools

Dresser	Paintbrushes: 3-inch-wide flat and #10
Sandpaper	artist's brushes
Tack cloth	Pencil and paper
Latex primer	Stencils (optional)
Latex enamel paint in desired colors	Low-tack painter's tape
	Polyurethane

1 Lightly sand the dresser top, sides, and drawers; wipe with a tack cloth. Prime the surfaces; let dry.

2 Paint the dresser body with two coats of enamel paint.

3 Sketch the patterns you want to use on paper first. Use elements in the room—fabrics, rugs, artwork—for inspiration. (Or buy stencils in the desired shapes.)

4 Paint each drawer the desired base color; let dry. Using a pencil and a light touch, draw the designs onto the drawers. For uneven checks and dots like the ones *opposite,* paint freehand over the pencil lines using a #10 artist's brush. For a more even pattern and straighter lines, use low-tack painter's tape to mask off the areas that will receive paint. More uniform dots can be made with a stencil or by dipping the end of a dowel or the eraser end of a pencil into the paint and pressing it onto the drawer.

5 Seal the painted surfaces with two coats of polyurethane, allowing time for it to dry between coats.

hot tip

Painted furniture is especially appealing in nurseries and younger children's bedrooms. Colorful paints and fanciful designs delight youngsters and parents alike.

buy it unfinished for less

If you're willing to assemble and finish wooden pieces, you'll save 20 percent to 60 percent off regular prices. What's more, you'll be able to customize the colors and designs to match your decor.

Plan the painting scheme and then paint each piece before assembly. It's much easier to paint the pieces separately than to work your brush into small spaces.

Use low-tack painter's tape to keep the colors separate as you paint. If you want to give preassembled furniture a multicolor paint treatment, note where pieces join, such as the posts and sides on a crib, the drawer fronts on a dresser, or the top and legs of a table. Then plan your design with these natural divisions in mind.

Grooves, overlays, or routed edges also lend themselves to color breaks. Look around the room for other pieces that can be painted in the same manner. Paint picture frames to match a headboard or window trim to match a color in the rug. Creativity is key.

TOOL TALK Depending on the paint job, you may need everything from basic paintbrushes to specialty-finish brushes and tools, *opposite.* Always buy the best brushes you can afford. Add a level, straightedge, and low-tack painter's tape to your supply list.

THE PRICE IS RIGHT Look for unfinished particleboard bedside or occasional tables similar to the ones, *below,* at home discount stores for $6–$25. Paint them with animal images or colorful polka dots and checks.

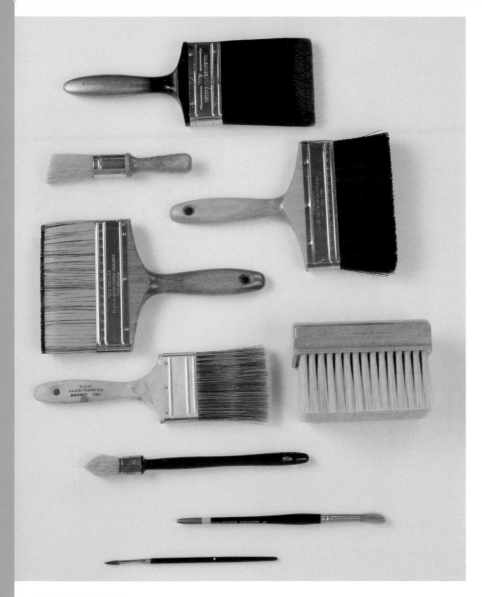

If you're using latex (water-base) paint, choose brushes with nylon bristles or a nylon/polyester blend. Use a large, flat brush (nonangled) for fast application when painting walls and large surfaces. Use angled brushes for trims and moldings.

how to
paint like a pro

Schedule your painting project for a time when you will have several consecutive days free to work on it. For small projects, you may need only a few hours a day to do the painting; however, you'll also need to allow time for each coat of paint to dry. In addition, you'll have to complete various preparatory steps before you start painting.

1. Repair damaged areas on the walls or furniture before painting. Ensure that the surfaces are clean, smooth, and dry before you apply paint.
2. Paint color combinations on a practice board first. Put the board in the room and live with it for a few days, observing it in different lights and at different times of the day.
3. If you're applying a glaze, combing, or doing a more complicated technique in a large room, it's best to work with a partner to avoid breaks in the pattern. One person can successfully paint below a chair rail, above a mantel, or on a single wall, but you'll need help if you're painting a larger area.
4. Dampen your brush with water before painting with latex (water-base) products. This helps keep paint from quickly accumulating and drying out the bristles, and makes cleanup easier.
5. Step back from the wall several times during each stage of the work to get a sense of the composition as a whole.

What could be more fun than accessorizing a baby's, child's, or teen's room? Inexpensive accents abound at garage sales, thrift shops, and home discount centers. Before you go bargain-hunting, page through this chapter for ideas on how to make a ho-hum room a hot property without breaking the bank.

Other ideas for tiebacks include gluing ribbon to the back of a tiny baby book ($1 at dollar stores or about $6 at bookstores). You also could use cute baby headbands (less than $5 at children's discount clothing stores) or colorful A-B-C blocks ($8 for a set of 26 letters at toy stores) glued to trims that coordinate with the colors of the room.

make baby-shoe tiebacks

Materials

Baby shoes
Extra long shoelaces

Stick-on or screw-in cup hooks

1 Buy tiny tennis shoes in a color that coordinates with your baby's room and lace them with extra long shoelaces.
2 Tie the laces of the shoes in a loose knot close to the shoes, leaving long strings.
3 Hold tiebacks up to the wall to determine the best placement.
4 Install stick-on or screw-in cup hooks at the spots where you want to attach the tiebacks to the wall.
5 Tie the shoelaces into loose bows around the curtains and loop the strings over the cup hooks.

TINY TIEBACKS Use baby shoes ($1 a pair at dollar stores; up to $12 a pair at home discount centers) as tiebacks for curtains to add color and personality to a newborn's room, *opposite*.

hot tip

Heirlooms and
antiques make great
one-of-a-kind
touches for any
child's room.
Vintage baby
clothes, hats, and
quilts, as well as old
toys, collections,
and artwork add
character and
charm. Even
timeworn baby
plates can function
as art when nicely
arranged on a wall.

enjoy a thrifty tea for two

Remember playing with tea sets as a child? Add a secondhand table and two chairs to your child's room to set the stage for hours of make-believe. Then a little one can have teatime with a stuffed animal or a young friend.

Make a display of favorite toys from your childhood to create a vintage feel in the nursery—at no cost. Or hang vintage baby and children's hats you have in storage or look for them at thrift shops and secondhand stores. Hide flaws or worn areas by arranging the items strategically.

TEA, ANYONE? Mismatched cups and tea servers sell for less than $5 each at thrift shops and garage sales. Home discount stores offer child-size tea sets for $15 or less, *opposite.*

use low-cost, everyday items

Part of the fun of decorating kids' rooms is using everyday items in a surprising way. For example, plain old clothespins can spiff up a white table, *right,* with texture and style. For a different look, tack on rocks, buttons, or faux gemstones instead of clothespins.

TABLE IT A small flea-market table, *above,* costs $25 or less. The old-fashioned clothespins are only $4 for a bag of 40, and the spray paint and sealer together cost about $6. For about $35, you'll have an unusual table that will make you proud to say, "I made it myself."

embellish a table

Materials and Tools

Small secondhand table	Clothespins
Sandpaper	White acrylic spray paint
Hot-glue gun and glue sticks	Spray-on sealer for wood

1 Purchase a secondhand table and sand it. Then hot-glue the clothespins around the tabletop.
2 Spray-paint the table white; let dry.
3 Seal with a spray-on sealer to protect the surface; let dry.

stir in some surprise

One of the best things about decorating kids' rooms is that you're free to indulge your playful side. Kids love wild ideas, so go ahead—get crazy with ordinary items and give them a stylish surprise. Make a secondhand wagon into a bedside table, *opposite,* or hang a colorful hammock to hold stuffed animals. Put small toys in an upside-down 10-gallon hat to complete a carefree Western theme.

Most of these items can be found at flea markets, secondhand stores or estate sales, and while you're there, you'll probably pick up a few more items and ideas.

GOT WHEELS? A used wagon, *opposite,* takes on a new life as a bedside table. You may find a similar one for around $30.

RAINY-DAY FUN Sky blue walls, a hanging yellow slicker, and a curtain accent a closet with a clever little reading nook, *below.*

hot tip

In a child's or teen's room, add a touch of elegance above a bed by draping fabric suspended from the ceiling. Choose lightweight, breathable fabrics that are easy to launder. Purchase a ready-made sheer scarf valance or fabric long enough to extend from the ceiling to the floor and back again. Tie a loose knot in the center of the scarf and attach it to the ceiling with cup hooks. Puddle the excess fabric on the floor.

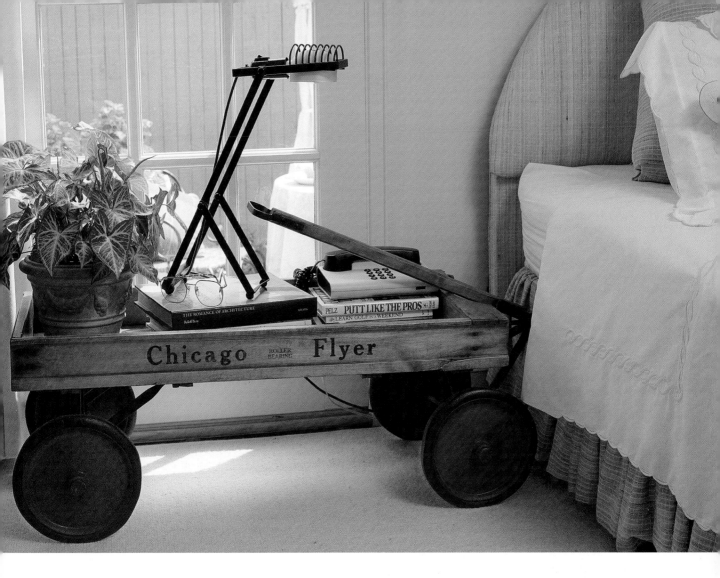

no-cost ideas for kids' rooms

Sometimes it costs nothing to give a kid's room that special something. Here are a few ideas.

- **Use free artwork.** Your local library may have artwork that can be checked out for a few weeks or months. So switch out the artwork in your kids' rooms often; it's a great way for them to learn about various artists. Discuss the artists' lives and works together.

cheap thrills

- **Repurpose items.** Ever watch the home makeover shows on TV? Often the transformation begins with a treasure the homeowner has—something tucked away in an attic or basement. Look around your home and move things around. Find a piece that's been in the background and bring it into the spotlight.
- **Display collections.** Pull out those dusty collectibles—plates, spoons, seashells, or vintage postcards—and create an interesting arrangement.
- **Let 'em paint.** If you're ready for a real adventure, let your kids decorate one wall in their rooms. Get out old, leftover paint. Arm the kids with some old squirt guns and drape off a wall that they can "attack" with colors. They'll have a blast, and you'll end up with colorful, modern art they'll be proud to say they created.
- **Decorate with sheets,** blankets, and quilts. Use them as a backdrop for pictures or hang them as a headboard. They can function as slipcovers, tablecloths, or canopies—or whatever your imagination suggests.
- **Highlight treasured photos.** Black and white pictures can be dramatic, while vividly colored ones can coordinate with the hues in the room. No matter how casual the family moment, capture it on film and display the results for lasting enjoyment.

save at dollar stores

When you're looking for inexpensive projects to make, check out the dollar stores popping up all over the country. For example the plain galvanized watering can, *below,* from a dollar store becomes a vase when it's dressed up in bright flowers. Plastic watering cans, which may cost less than metal ones, work equally well when you spray-paint them to match your decor.

Dollar stores are a good source for candles and lampshades like the ones used in the projects, *opposite.* If what you need isn't in stock the first time, check back later. Inventory changes often, sometimes daily.

A BLOOMING VASE FOR UNDER $10 A watering can, *below,* costs only about $1–$4 at dollar stores, spray paint is $2 at home centers, and flower stickers or fabric trims cost less than $4 at hobby stores.

dress up a watering can

Materials and Tools

Watering can
Spray paint
Hot-glue gun and glue sticks
Paper flower stickers or flower fabric trim
Fresh or artificial flowers

1 Pick up a watering can at a garage sale or a dollar store and spray-paint it a bright color.
2 Hot-glue flower stickers or flower fabric trim to the can.
3 Fill the can with water and fresh flowers from your garden or use artificial blooms.

how to
create an iced candle

Materials

Pillar candle
Square glass dish
1–3 strands of crystal-like beads
Straight pins

1　Place the candle in the center of the dish.
2　Wrap a bead strand around the candle, knotting it in the front.
3　Use pins to hold the bead strands in place, pinning the beads on the backside of the candle.
4　Arrange more beads on the candle and in the dish as desired.

GO WITH THE GLOW The beautiful iced candle and tray, *above,* cost only $6. That's $1 for the candle, $3 for the beads, $1 for the square dish, and $1 for straight pins.

LIGHT IT UP A plain lampshade ($12 at home discount stores) and colorful fabric remnants ($2–$5) pair up for instant personality, *below.*

how to
create a patchwork lampshade

Materials and Tools

Plain lampshade
Hot-glue gun and glue sticks
Colorful stickers or fabric

1　Buy a solid-color, smooth lampshade to fit a lamp you have.
2　Using a hot-glue gun adhere the pieces of fabric to the lampshade.
3　Allow the glue on the lampshade to dry thoroughly before turning on the lamp.

Caution: Lampshades sitting close to a bulb may get very warm. Use nonflammable papers and glues that can withstand moderate heat. Use high-temperature glue guns. Never use a higher-wattage lightbulb than the lamp manufacturer recommends.

how to
care for wicker

Keeping wicker clean takes a little effort because of the textured surface. Follow these steps to keep your wicker looking fresh and wonderful:

1. Vacuum the furniture regularly to prevent dust and dirt buildup or use a soft brush or feather duster.
2. Wipe down each piece occasionally, using a cloth dampened with water and mild detergent. Wring out your rag well to avoid making the wicker limp or soggy.
3. Cracking in wicker pieces usually is caused by dryness. Remedy this by a one-time application of boiled (not raw) linseed oil (use on painted pieces only). Apply it evenly over the piece, working the oil into the crevices.
4. Keep applying the linseed oil until the surface remains shiny, indicating that it is no longer absorbing the oil. Wipe off the excess oil with paper towels. Linseed oil is very flammable, so wet the used paper towels with water and wrap them tightly in plastic before putting them in the garbage.
5. Let the furniture dry at least 24 hours before adding any finishes.

hot tip

Age wicker artificially by brushing on a bright hue of paint and sanding or wiping some off while the paint is still tacky. Let dry and then repeat the process. Some areas will show raw wicker, while others will have subtle color.

win with thrifty wicker

Wicker made its first splash in the 14th century B.C. when the baby Moses made his safe passage on the river Nile in a wicker basket woven from reeds. Wicker is as functional now as it was then—and fashionable too, whether you're decorating a baby's, child's, or teen's space.

Wicker is easy to maintain and mixes well with other casual furniture. Combine wicker with other natural materials, such as cotton quilts, woven baskets, and sisal rugs, for a cozy, down-home feeling.

Wicker furniture is affordable even when purchased new. Finding wicker treasures at garage sales or thrift shops is even more thrifty and gives you the opportunity to be creative with paint.

Add a little romance to a wicker chair by hot-gluing fringe and tassels to the bottom, back, and sides. For a breezy, natural style, adorn wicker chairs with cushions and throws. Whether it's stained or painted, your wicker will warm up the room and give the space a nostalgic feel.

WICKER IN THE WORKS The combination of fresh white wicker and cheerful pillows, *above left,* brings breezy spring days to mind.

WICKER ROCKS A stylish wicker rocker, *above,* or chair, *left,* is a classic accent that brings a touch of comfort and class to a baby's nursery. Use it again in a child's or teen's room, spray-painting it, if needed, to fit in with the decor.

find low-cost headboards

A patchwork quilt makes an effective headboard in almost any kid's room, whether it's a nursery or a teen hangout. Although antique quilts are expensive, twin-size replicas are available at home discount stores for $25 to $35.

To hang the quilt, hand-sew a fabric pocket along the top back edge of the quilt. Make the pocket large enough to accommodate a wood dowel ($1 to $4 at home improvement centers) that can be hung from hooks on the wall. Or hang the quilt directly over the dowel if it's long enough to drape down the wall. Here are several other inexpensive headboard ideas.

- **Use sections of wrought iron** ($30 or less) or picket fence (around $10) from flea markets to make a great headboard.
- **Hang a Shaker-style peg rack** (less than $25 at most home improvement stores) above the head of the bed and outfit the rack with vintage hats or other accessories.
- **Drape a square piece of material** in your child's favorite color above the bed. With tacks, attach colorful artwork he or she made.

QUILT POWER The colorful quilt, *opposite*, serves as an inexpensive headboard and a piece of artwork. It gives a homey feeling to the room. Choose a quilt with darker colors or bold primary colors to create a more traditionally masculine look.

IRON IT A painted iron headboard, *above*, joins the color parade. Look for similar iron pieces—unpainted—at flea markets or thrift shops. Then spruce up your find with primer and paint made especially for metal.

WILD WILD WEST Western themes are usually popular with boys and teens. Accessorize with simple bandanna window treatments, used cowboy boots, and pre-owned equestrian gear.

round up the savings

When decorating for boys and teens, let sturdy be your watchword. Boys generally like a rugged look, and you'll appreciate furniture that lasts through their childhood and teen years.

Beyond furniture, search for accessories—tough textiles and practical gear—that reinforce the rugged theme. If your youngster can't leave home without a 10-gallon hat and cowboy boots, this log cabin room, *left,* may inspire you. Here's how to create casual Western style:

- **Drape plaid blankets** at the window for an Old West look ($3–$7 at garage sales).
- **Corral curtains with tiebacks made** of rope ($2 at hobby stores). Or cinch up a valance with old Western belts ($1–$3 at garage sales).
- **Hang a barn sash** (about $30 at farm auctions) as a mirror in the room.
- **Use cowboy boots** ($3–$10 at garage sales) as plant holders or containers for small toys.
- **Display an old saddle** or other used equestrian gear ($10–$45 at farm auctions) on the wall to add Western twang.

hot tip

If you and your child or teen like this look, visit Western-apparel stores for inspiration. The displays in the store and the store windows may trigger a decorating idea, such as a lampshade with Wild West postcards, or tumbleweeds in a cowboy boot.

how to

make a Western window treatment

Materials

Tree branch or log	Thread
Pack of tie-on bandannas	Blinds or shades for additional privacy (optional)

1. Find a fallen tree branch, log, or sturdy twig in your backyard or local park and hang it over the window as a curtain rod. (Spray it for insects before bringing it inside your home.)
2. Stitch the bandannas together, either by hand or machine, to serve as the valance or curtain. Or drape them individually over the branch for a casual, spirited look.
3. If you like the tab-top curtains, *opposite,* cut 6-inch-long strips of fabric and attach them (wrong sides facing) at 6- to 8-inch intervals along the top of the curtain. Then knot them over the branch curtain rod. (Fabrics don't slide very well on natural rods like this, so you may want to add blinds or shades for more privacy.)

FOR THE BIRDS The cute table, *above,* is made from a used birdbath pedestal (about $15–$20 at garage sales or thrift shops) and a piece of round glass purchased at a home center for $12. Add flowers and botanical books for a casual look.

ADD SOME FUN Funky wall art, such as the secondhand "Love" sign, *opposite,* adds a cheerful, offbeat attitude that goes well with outdoor furniture.

hot tip

If your child or teen loves the outdoors, consider decorating with accessories such as a butterfly net (about $12), sporting gear, or a collection of used gardening tools (about $7 each at auctions or tag sales). Look in seed and camping catalogs to get ideas; professional photographers often use props that could inspire you.

use outdoor furniture

The rugged, casual style of outdoor furniture is a perfect fit for seating areas in teens' rooms. The pieces are a bargain too: Used outdoor chairs, metal or wooden gliders, or wooden chairs sell for $5–$45 at garage sales or thrift shops.

If the surface is scratched or has minor dents, a quick coat of spray paint will hide the flaws and help the pieces fit in with the room decor. Add lots of plants and a few unique wall pieces, such as vintage gardening tools or signs, and you'll have a casual conversation area that invites teens to rest and relax.

Another plus: As teens grow up and move out, these pieces can move to the porch, sunroom, or patio.

hot tip

Help your kids choose something to collect so antiquing can become a fun family event. Depending on your child's age, you may want to start with unbreakables such as wooden blocks or plastic construction toys. Brainstorm together to decide how to display these items.

chalk up those savings

Here's a novel way to encourage kids or teens to be creative. Paint a wall or part of a wall with chalkboard paint (about $10 a quart at most home centers and crafts stores). Then your kids can draw, doodle, or write to their hearts' content, without your having to clean up after them.

One coat of chalkboard paint covers most surfaces and dries overnight. Manufacturers offer a spectrum of colors to match the theme and decor you have in mind.

SPARK THEIR CREATIVITY Chalkboard paint can make almost any space into a play zone, *below*. Teens can write notes on the wall in the study area, *opposite*.

teach your kids money skills with decorating projects

- **Decide how much you can spend** on the decorating project before you meet with your kids.
- **Together choose a theme** for the room and determine which new items and supplies need to be purchased. To come up with ideas, flip through some current decorating books and magazines.
- **Split up the list** of needed supplies and items. Have each person involved research where to get supplies for the least cost, and ask everyone to write down how much each item will cost.
- **Get together and see whether the list fits the budget.** If the total is over the budgeted amount discuss which items your kids can live without or look together for a less expensive place to get them.
- **Stick to the budget.** Part of teaching your children to be financially responsible is to avoid automatically spending more. If they want a more expensive item or an extra item that blows the budget, offer a compromise. Let them pay that amount from their allowance or from money they make doing extra chores around the house.

cheap thrills

MAKE IT ACCESSIBLE The low built-in bookcase with smooth edges, *above,* provides safe, easy storage for kids. Freestanding corner units work equally well and cost about $30 at home discount centers. Paint one to match the room decor.

how to

make a crate desk

Materials and Tools

Sandpaper	Paint
6×2-foot piece of	Paintbrush
wood, ½ inch thick	4 plastic crates

1 Sand the edges of the wood to remove roughness. Paint and let dry.
2 Stack the crates as shown and place the wood on top.

store it on the cheap

Can you see the floor in your kids' rooms? If clutter has taken over, conquer it with these storage solutions:

- **Shoeboxes** (free after you have been out shopping) store building blocks, small cars, and various other small toys.
- **Tote bags** (under $5) help kids transport toys from one room to another, cutting down on spills and "toy litter" throughout the house.
- **Large plastic tubs** ($10 at most home improvement stores) can hold train sets, car tracks, assorted sports gear, and a variety of doll accessories.
- **Flat, under-the-bed boxes** ($10 for plastic ones) store out-of-season toys such as kites and baseball gear.

- **Hat racks** (less than $25) make wonderful hooks for stuffed animals, book bags, and backpacks.
- **Toy hammocks** ($10 at large chain retail stores) hold stuffed animals.
- **A colorful shower curtain rod** ($10) wrapped with hook-and-loop tape ($3 for a pack of 12 strips) can keep stuffed animals from creeping underfoot.

A DESK THAT GROWS The desktop, *below,* is perfect for putting together puzzles and for coloring. As your child matures, remove the center baskets to turn the unit into a teen's desk complete with handy storage on each side of the kneehole.

Insist that your kids toss out something old every time they add something to their rooms. That way you'll keep clutter at bay so it doesn't accumulate into a daunting pile.

let the treasure hunt begin!

You've got style. You've got imagination. You want your kids' rooms to reflect that—and to reflect the kids' personalities. However, like most people you probably don't have an unlimited amount of money for decorating. That's why you need to become a Brave Bargain Hunter.

You'll save money, and you'll end up with one-of-a-kind decorating items no one else has. And if you go with a friend or take the kids along, the shopping experience itself can be loads of fun. Here are some venues you might want to visit:

- **Garage and tag sales.** From used kids' furniture to vintage stuffed animals, you'll find items for your decorating projects. And you may be able to bargain, especially if the sale is winding down.

- **Consignment shops.** These used to offer mainly clothes. Now many include home furnishings in good condition for about half the price of new items. If you'd like to bring items to sell, ask about the policies, including which days items are accepted and how much of the selling price consigners get (40 percent to 60 percent is common).
- **Flea markets.** These can be a great place for bargains such as old doors, kids' dolls, miniature and regular-size quilts, and vintage fabrics. Some dealers welcome negotiations; some don't. Usually a sign saying "Prices Firm" means don't dicker.
- **Swapping.** Ask around among your friends or colleagues at work or church. They may have secondhand furniture that's gathering dust, such as a bassinet or crib they'll never use or vintage suitcases you could use to make a coffee table. You could offer to trade some of your decorating overflow items for theirs.
- **Online shopping sites.** Sites selling used and discount household furnishings are becoming increasingly popular. Here are a few to check out:
  - ebay.com
  - bizrate.com
  - lx.direct.com
  - furniturefind.com
  - AllDorm.com
  - CollegiateMall.com
- **Thrift shops,** such as The Salvation Army, Goodwill, and Disabled American Veterans. From vintage and retro clothing to bedspreads, from flower urns to side tables, you'll discover a wealth of items to lend pizzazz to your kids' rooms.
- **Estate sales and auctions.** These usually are advertised in local papers and sometimes include a "preview" day when shoppers can look over what's going to be offered.
- **"Scratch-and-dent" sales** in local furniture stores. Often pieces labeled "damaged" have minimal flaws, that can be camouflaged with a little paint or colorful cushions. Make an offer—if the item has been on the floor a long time, you could get an even lower price.

- **Import shops.** These stores offer pieces with exotic style. If your child or teen is interested in Africa or Asia, you're in luck. Import shops carry many pieces from these continents, so you'll be able to build a decorating theme in an instant. These shops are also a great source for colorful candles, embellished pillows, and unique wall sconces.
- **Classified ads** in shoppers or newspapers. These may advertise used furniture at low prices, often because of a death in the family, a divorce, or an unexpected move.

WHEN YOU SHOP at flea markets or auctions, *opposite and left,* go early to check out all the offerings. Write down the items you're interested in and note which booths and where they're located. That way, you'll know right where to go when you're ready to buy.

how to shop online auctions

- **You'll need a computer**, a modem with a speed of at least 28.8K (56.6K is preferred), and access to the Internet with a service provider such as America Online.
- **Access online auction sites** by typing the World Wide Web address in the box at the top of the screen. Or choose a search engine such as Google and type in "flea markets," "discount furniture," or "bargain furnishings."
- **Hundreds of listings will appear.** If you find one you like, highlight it as a favorite.
- **Read the site's auction rules carefully.** Some have tutorials that guide you through the process. Generally you find a description of the item up for sale, the current or starting price, the number of bids posted, and the time the auction closes.
- **Many of these sites have a buyer feedback area** that provides you with information on the seller—that's a good thing to check out before you bid.
- **To place a bid**, register with the auction house and receive a user ID and password. Once you have placed a bid, it's a binding contract. If your bid is accepted, most auction houses notify you by e-mail.
- **You and the seller need to arrange** for shipping and payment. You'll need to pay for the shipping, taxes, and insurance. You may also be charged a buyer's fee of up to 10 percent.
- **Pay by check or credit card**, never cash.

cheap thrills

index

Find Your Style

Better Homes and Gardens

color schemes made easy

Better Homes and Gardens. decorating ideas under $50

quick updates to what you already own

Better Homes and Gardens. childstyle Decorating Ideas & Projects For Kids' Rooms

Better Homes and Gardens. Style By The Aisle OFF-THE-RACK DECORATING FOR AFFORD

new decorating book Better Homes and Gardens

The elements of your style...
can be found in great decorating books from
Better Homes and Gardens®—wherever books are sold.